T0317588

Volatility

Founded in 1807, John Wiley & Sons is the oldest independent publishing company in the United States. With offices in North America, Europe, Australia and Asia, Wiley is globally committed to developing and marketing print and electronic products and services for our customers' professional and personal knowledge and understanding.

The Wiley Finance series contains books written specifically for finance and investment professionals as well as sophisticated individual investors and their financial advisors. Book topics range from portfolio management to e-commerce, risk management, financial engineering, valuation and financial instrument analysis, as well as much more.

For a list of available titles, visit our Web site at www.WileyFinance .com.

Volatility

Practical Options Theory

ADAM S. IQBAL

WILEY

Published by John Wiley & Sons, Inc., Hoboken, New Jersey.
Published simultaneously in Canada.

For general information on our other products and services or for technical support, please contact our Customer Care Department within the United States at (800) 762–2974, outside the United States at (317) 572–3993, or fax (317) 572–4002.

Wiley publishes in a variety of print and electronic formats and by print-on-demand. Some material included with standard print versions of this book may not be included in e-books or in print-on-demand. If this book refers to media such as a CD or DVD that is not included in the version you purchased, you may download this material at http://booksupport.wiley.com. For more information about Wiley products, visit www.wiley.com.

Library of Congress Cataloging-in-Publication Data

Names: Iqbal, Adam S., 1983- author.
Title: Volatility : practical options theory / by Adam S. Iqbal.
Description: Hoboken, New Jersey : John Wiley & Sons, Inc., [2018] | Series: Wiley finance | Includes bibliographical references and index. |
Identifiers: LCCN 2018012654 (print) | LCCN 2018013434 (ebook) | ISBN 9781119501671 (pdf) | ISBN 9781119501688 (epub) | ISBN 9781119501619 (cloth)
Subjects: LCSH: Options (Finance) | Securities--Prices--Mathematical models.
Classification: LCC HG6024.A3 (ebook) | LCC HG6024.A3 I72 2018 (print) | DDC 332.64/5301--dc23
LC record available at https://lccn.loc.gov/2018012654

Cover Design: Wiley
Cover Image: © enjoynz / iStockphoto

Printed and bound by CPI Group (UK) Ltd, Croydon, CR0 4YY

C9781119501619_120124

To Mum, Dad, my wife, Gosia, and my beautiful one-year-old daughter, Maria, without whom this book would have been finished up to one year earlier.

Contents

CHAPTER 5
The Basic Greeks: Vega **87**
    5.1   Vega   88
    5.2   Understanding Vega via the PDF   89
    5.3   Understanding Vega via Gamma Trading   89
    5.4   Vega of an ATMS Option Across Tenors   90
    5.5   Vega and Spot   91
    5.6   Dependence of Vega on Implied Volatility   94
    5.7   Vega Profiles Applied in Practical Options Trading   95
    5.8   Vega and PnL Explain   96
    5.9   Trader's Summary   97

CHAPTER 6
Implied Volatility and Term Structure **99**
    6.1   Implied Volatility, $\sigma_{implied}$ 100
    6.2   Term Structure   104
    6.3   Flat Vega and Weighted Vega Greeks   104
        6.3.1   *Flat Vega*   105
        6.3.2   *Weighted Vega*   106
        6.3.3   *Beta-Weighted Vega*   108
    6.4   Forward Volatility, Forward Variance, and Term
          Volatility   108
        6.4.1   *Calculating Implied Forward Volatility*   110
    6.5   Building a Term Structure Model Using Daily Forward
          Volatility   111
    6.6   Setting Base Volatility Using a Three-Parameter
          GARCH Model   114
        6.6.1   *Applying the Three-Parameter Model*   116
        6.6.2   *Limitations of GARCH*   117
        6.6.3   *Risk Management Using the Three-Parameter*
              Model   118
        6.6.4   *Empirical GARCH Estimation*   118
    6.7   Volatility Carry and Forward Volatility Agreements   119
        6.7.1   *Volatility Carry in the GARCH Model*   120
        6.7.2   *Common Pitfalls in Volatility Carry Trading*   121
    6.8   Trader's Summary   121

CHAPTER 7
Vanna, Risk Reversal, and Skewness **123**
    7.1   Risk Reversal   125
    7.2   Skewness   127

Preface

This book studies options, the financial contracts that provide exposure to volatility. It has one main objective.

While there already exist several excellent references on the mathematical theory underlying options (Shreve, 2000, Duffie, 2001, and Bjork, 2009) are examples among a list too long to complete here), there is a relative absence of texts that attempt to explain how to bring the many theoretical ideas into practice. The main objective in this book is to provide an intuitive, as well as technical, understanding of both the basic and advanced ideas in options theory, with the aim of encouraging translational work from theory into practical application by market makers, portfolio managers, investment managers, risk managers, traders, and other market practitioners.

I show the reader that several of the most important concepts in options theory such as implied volatility, delta hedging, time value, and many of the so-called *option Greeks* can be understood by appealing to intuitive economic arguments alone, without the need to build a formal mathematical model. Once this knowledge is in place, I go on to explain the seminal Black-Scholes-Merton mathematical model. The reader will understand how the model-free approach and mathematical models are related to each other, their underlying theoretical assumptions, and their implications to a level that facilitates their practical implementation.

The approach taken in this book may prove valuable to options traders and other practitioners tasked with making pricing or risk management decisions in an environment where time constraints mean that simplicity and intuition are of greater value than mathematical formalism. This approach may also prove useful to academics interested in the translational process of theoretical options pricing into practical application, and in the feedback loop between academia and practice.

The majority of the concepts in this text are applicable to options on equities, bonds, and commodities. However, this book provides in-depth insight into the theoretical and practical function of the FX options over-the-counter (OTC) market. Given the liquidity in FX spot (and forwards) markets and the lower number of trading constraints (such as short selling; selling EUR-USD is the same as buying USD-EUR), FX markets arguably provide one of the better opportunities to implement the theoretical ideas presented here.

The target audience for this book includes, but is not limited to, industry practitioners, finance and economics advanced undergraduate and graduate students, MBA students, and academics interested in translational finance. I presume some exposure to undergraduate level probability, statistics, and calculus. However, this should not deter readers with less exposure to these topics for at least two reasons. First, the presentation is consciously informal with the aim of exposing ideas in their simplest form before going back and understanding their foundations. Second, I provide several mathematical appendices to assist such readers and to keep this book self-contained with respect to the most important concepts. Although at times it may not seem to be the case, the challenges in successful options trading are conceptual rather than mathematical.

Acknowledgments

This book owes a debt to the many colleagues in FX options I have worked with over my years at Goldman Sachs and Barclays Investment Bank for their engagement in our discussions about options theory and for all that they have taught me.

I also thank the people who have taken time to provide comments, proofreading, and feedback. In particular, I thank Kimiya Minoukadeh, Mobeen Iqbal, and Christopher Cullen for their efforts. All remaining errors are my own.

About the Author

Adam S. Iqbal is a Managing Director and Global Head of FX Exotics and Correlation at Goldman Sachs, where he has also served as EMEA Head of G10 FX Options Trading, running several FX vanilla and exotic long-, and short-dated options portfolios. Previously, he was an FX Volatility Portfolio Manager at Pimco. He has also worked as a vanilla and exotic options trader at Barclays Investment Bank in London. He holds a PhD in financial mathematics and financial economics from Imperial College London, an MSc in applied mathematics from Oxford University, and an MSci, MA, and BA in theoretical physics from Cambridge University. Dr. Iqbal has held a visiting academic position at Imperial College London and has guest lectured at the London School of Economics. He lives in London with his wife, Malgorzata, and their one-year-old daughter, Maria.

Volatility

CHAPTER 1

Volatility and Options

*V*olatility is a measure of the uncertainty of the future price of a security. Options are contracts that allow market participants to expose their portfolios to the future volatility of an underlying security. The buyer of an option is said to be *long volatility* because she expects to profit if volatility rises. The converse is true for the seller of an option. She is *short volatility*.

Although options are often also simultaneously used for other purposes, such as to gain exposure to the direction in which the underlying security will move, to the future path of interest rates, or to gain leverage, among other uses, their raison d'etre is that they allow market participants to trade volatility. Indeed, forwards (or futures) already allow market participants to expose their portfolios to direction, to interest rates, and to gain leverage. We explore the other joint uses of options over the course of this book. However, the aim in this chapter is to provide a broad understanding of the concept of volatility and to communicate the central idea that an option is a bet on future volatility.

The exposition in this chapter is deliberately imprecise in order to disseminate the intuition underlying options theory and practical options trading more quickly. We will study these topics in depth and with greater accuracy in later chapters.

1.1   WHAT IS AN OPTION?

Perhaps the quickest and most intuitive way to understand the basics of options is through inspecting their payoff profiles. The payoff profiles of a *vanilla* call option and put option are shown in Figure 1.1. I explain these diagrams in more detail in Chapter 2. For now, the important points to understand are:

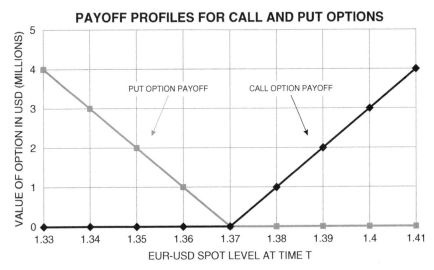

FIGURE 1.1 The black and gray lines show the payoff profiles of a call and put option respectively. In this example, the payoff corresponds to an option with notional of 100 million EUR and a strike of 1.37. The horizontal axis shows the level of EUR-USD at the maturity, or expiry, time of the option. If EUR-USD is above (below) 1.37 on the expiry date of the option, the owner of the call (put) can buy (sell) 100 million EUR-USD at 1.37 if they so choose. In FX markets, the expiry date typically ranges from overnight through to 20 years, although even longer expiries are possible. The vertical axis shows the payoff to the owner of the option in USD. The payoff of the call option is zero if EUR-USD is below 1.37 at the expiry time because the trader would not rationally exercise her option to buy EUR-USD at the higher price of 1.37. However, it is positive if EUR-USD is above 1.37 and rises linearly. The put option behaves similarly, but the payoff is zero if EUR-USD is above 1.37, and positive if EUR-USD is below 1.37.

■ The payoffs depend on the value of an underlying security (the EUR–USD exchange rate in the example in Figure 1.1[1]) at the expiry time. We can rephrase this; the payoff is *derived* from the value of EUR-USD. This is why options are members of a class of financial products called *derivatives*.

---

[1]Readers unfamiliar with quotation conventions in foreign exchange should understand the EUR–USD exchange rate as the number of USD per EUR. For example, EUR-USD at 1.37 means 1.37 USD exchange for 1 EUR. Note that equities are quoted analogously. Microsoft stock trading at 100 USD means Microsoft-USD is 100.

- The call (put) option allows the trader to buy (sell) the underlying security at a prespecified price, called the strike price (EUR-USD at 1.37 in our example) on the expiry date.
- It follows that the payoff of the call option is $\max(S_T - K, 0) \times N$, where S_T is the price of the underlying security at the expiry of the option, K is the strike price, and N is the notional, or number of units of the option purchased. Suppose that the trader has purchased $N = 100$ million EUR of a $K = 1.37$ call option on EUR-USD. If $S_T = 1.39$, then the trader exercises her option and buys 100 million EUR at the strike price $K = 1.37$. She can then sell them in the market at $S_T = 1.39$ to receive $(1.39 - 1.37) \times 100$ million EUR = 2 million USD. However, if $S_T < 1.37$, then she can abandon her option and receive nothing. The formula $\max(S_T - K, 0) \times N$ correctly describes her payoff. Analogously, the put payoff is $\max(K - S_T, 0) \times N$.
- Note that the payoff is in USD in our example on EUR-USD. Had USD-JPY been the underlying currency pair, then the payoff would have been in JPY.
- The call payoff (black) is high when the value of the underlying asset is high. The put payoff (gray) is high when the value of the underlying asset is low. However, losses are floored in that the payoffs of both calls and puts are never negative, regardless of the value of the underlying. Options therefore provide insurance against market moves and their buyer must pay a premium.
- Purchasing a call (put) option is therefore a means to express the view that the underlying currency pair will rise (fall) and the maximum loss associated with this approach is the premium paid to purchase the option. However, we shall see that options and, in particular, portfolios of options, spot and forward positions, provide many ways of expressing these views and option traders do not in general buy calls (puts) to express the pure directional view that the underlying currency pair will rise (fall). Selecting the optimal portfolio requires a clear view on future volatility.
- Option payoffs are nonlinear and convex.

1.2   OPTIONS ARE BETS ON VOLATILITY

If the trader purchases both the call option and the put option, then her payoff profile is given by the V shape shown in Figure 1.2. This common strategy is called a *straddle*.

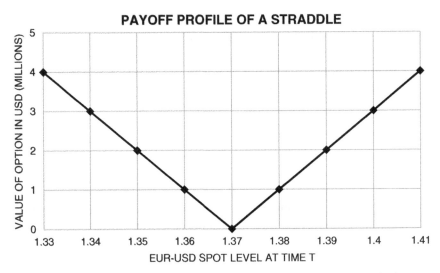

FIGURE 1.2 The figure shows the payoff of a straddle option strategy applied to EUR-USD. This is the purchase of a call option and a put option both with the same strike and notional. I use a strike $K = 1.37$, and notional $N = 100$ million EUR each. The horizontal axis shows the level of EUR-USD at the expiry time of the option. The vertical axis shows the payoff to the owner of the option in USD.

Unlike with individual calls and puts, it is clear that with a V-shaped symmetrical payoff profile the trader is not, initially at least, concerned as to whether the underlying security rises or falls because her payoff is the same if EUR-USD moves from 1.37 up to 1.39 or if it moves down to 1.35; in our example in Figure 1.2 it is 2 million USD in both cases. Her main concern is that EUR-USD moves away from 1.37. The further it moves, the higher her payoff. If EUR-USD were to stay at 1.37, then her payoff is zero and she loses the premium she paid to purchase the options. More so than any other option portfolio, the straddle makes clear that options are really bets on volatility. If EUR-USD volatility is high, then her chances of EUR-USD moving away from 1.37 and thereby earning a higher payoff are higher. For this reason, the buyer of the straddle is said to be *long volatility* and the seller is said to be *short volatility*.

One can show that individual call options and put options are also bets on volatility. Instead of the straddle, suppose that EUR-USD is trading at 1.37 and that the trader purchases a $K = 1.37$ EUR call option with $N = 200$ million EUR. The payoff of this position is shown in the left part of Figure 1.3. Simultaneously, the trader sells 100 million EUR-USD spot

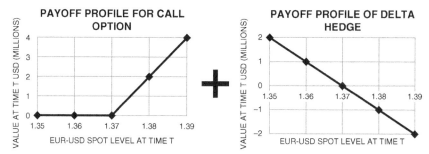

FIGURE 1.3 The left diagram shows the payoff of a call option with strike 1.37 and notional of 200 million EUR. The right diagram shows the payoff of selling 100 million EUR at 1.37. The payoff of the portfolio containing these two position is shown in Figure 1.4.

at 1.37. The payoff of this transaction is shown in the right-hand diagram in Figure 1.3. The selling of 100 million EUR-USD is called a *delta hedge*.[2] The payoff of the portfolio formed by purchasing the call option and executing the delta hedge is equivalent to that of a straddle (see Figure 1.4), with the notional of the call and the put each equaling 100 million EUR. Accordingly, a delta hedged call option is a straddle, which we have already established is a bet on volatility! An analogous result holds for the portfolio formed by purchasing the put option on EUR-USD and then delta hedging by purchasing EUR-USD spot.

We have shown that calls and puts are bets on volatility when the strike price is equal to the spot level (1.37 in our example). Such options are called *at-the-money spot*, or ATMS, options. In Chapter 9, I show that this argument is (locally) true for all options.

The discussion here goes some way toward convincing the reader that, despite the common usage of call and put options to bet on the direction in which the underlying security will move, the ability to delta hedge means that options are fundamentally not bets on direction, but are bets on volatility.

The example in this section also provides the reader with an early and intuitive introduction to the more general concept of delta hedging. Delta hedging means trading an amount of the underlying currency pair such that the options trader becomes indifferent to the direction in which spot moves.

---

[2]More precisely, the trader should sell 100 million of the EUR-USD forward contract to be *forward hedged*. More on forward hedging in later chapters.

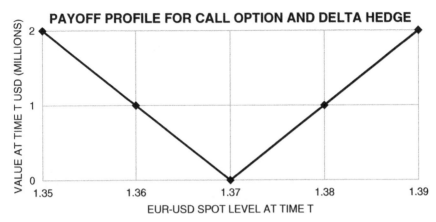

FIGURE 1.4   The figure shows the payoff formed from the purchase of a EUR-USD call option with strike 1.37 and notional of 200 million EUR, and selling 100 million EUR-USD at 1.37. The result is a straddle. Even though the trader purchased a call option, she is now indifferent to the direction in which EUR-USD moves, and is only concerned that the volatility is high so that the probability that EUR-USD moves away from 1.37 is high and she is able to collect a larger payoff.

1.3   OPTION PREMIUMS AND BREAKEVENS

Earlier, we established that the owner of the straddle requires the spot rate to move in order to profit (EUR-USD must move away from 1.37 in our example). An important question is, *how much* do we require spot to move so that the owner of the straddle is able to earn back the premium that she spent to purchase it? The points in spot space beyond which the payoff of the straddle is greater than the initial premium paid are called the *breakevens*. Let us investigate this idea further. The first step is to understand how option premiums are quoted.

1.3.1   Understanding Option Premiums

There are three main conventions in which option premiums are quoted. Again, let us take the example of a EUR-USD option.

% EUR   If the trader wishes to purchase the option using cash held in EUR, she may ask for a price in % EUR. Suppose that she is quoted a price of 0.75% EUR to purchase $N = 200$ million EUR of a $K = 1.38$ EUR-USD option. Then, quite simply, she must pay $0.75\% \times 200$ million EUR = 1.5 million EUR to purchase the option.

% USD If the trader wishes to pay the premium in USD, then she can ask for a price in % USD. Suppose EUR-USD spot is trading at 1.37. She will be quoted 0.745% USD to purchase the $K = 1.38$ option. The reason is that the USD notional of the option is 276 million USD. This is calculated based on the definition of a EUR-USD call option. By definition the trader may purchase 200 million EUR at 1.38 if she chooses. This is equivalent to selling 200 million EUR $\times$ 1.38 = 276 million USD. Her cost is therefore 0.745% $\times$ 276 million USD = 2.055 million USD, which is equivalent to 1.5 million EUR at the current spot rate of 1.37. Note that the price in % EUR and % USD are only equal if the strike equals the current spot level, and they are different otherwise.

USD Pips The third is USD pips. A *pip* or *price interest point* is loosely defined as the smallest price move that a given exchange rate makes based on market convention. So, for example, if EUR-USD moves from 1.3700 to 1.3710, we say that it has moved by 10 pips because market convention is to quote EUR-USD to four decimal places. However, if USDJPY moves from 115.50 to 115.60, then this is still 10 pips because market convention is to quote USD-JPY to two decimal places.

The USD pip price is defined by $N \times$ USD pip price = Cash price in USD, where N is the notional of the option in EUR. In the context of the example above, the USD pip price of the option is 102.75 USD pips. The reason is that 200 million EUR $\times$ 102.75 USD pips = 2.055 million USD.

A final important and related point to note is that option prices are most often quoted in terms of *Black-Scholes implied volatility*, which I denote by $\sigma_{implied}$. We shall study the meaning of $\sigma_{implied}$ in more detail later in the chapter and over the course of this book. At this stage, it is important for the reader to understand simply that it is the number that one must plug into a function (the Black-Scholes-Merton [BSM] function) to retrieve a premium price in one of the three conventions described previously.

1.3.2 Relation Between Premium and Breakeven

One may ask, why have the quoting conventions described earlier developed as they have? There are at least two reasons.

First, and very plainly, quoting in terms of % of notional or pips is convenient because it takes the option notional out of the discussion, whereas a cash price is tied to a given notional.

Second, and more important in the context of practical options trading, is that thinking in terms of % or pips allows the option trader to perform instant *rule-of-thumb* analysis on the option that she is considering buying or selling. Consider, for example, the 1.38 strike call option priced at 102.75 USD pips earlier. The trader knows that her breakeven is therefore 1.390275.

Next, consider the 1.37 strike straddle. Suppose that the spot rate is 1.37, the cost of the 1.37 EUR-USD call option is 0.5% USD, and the cost of the 1.37 put option is also 0.5% USD. The trader purchases both options. She buys notional N EUR of the call and N EUR of the put. The total cost in USD is therefore 1% of $N \times 1.37$. The trader therefore requires spot to move away from 1.37 by 1% in order to break even because if spot moves higher to 1.3837, she makes 1% on notional $1.37N$ and similarly if spot moves lower to 1.3563. Figure 1.5 assumes $N = 100$ million EUR and makes this point clear.

Equivalently, the price of the straddle in USD pips is 68.5 for the call and 68.5 for the put. Therefore the total is 137 USD pips, to give breakevens of 1.3563 and 1.3837.

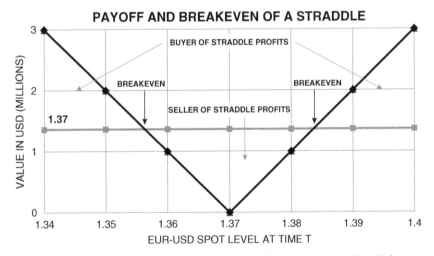

FIGURE 1.5 The trader has purchased 100 million EUR each of the call and the put. This is equivalent to 137 million USD each of the call and the put. The cost is 1.37 million USD, or 1%. The trader's breakeven is therefore 1%. We see from the diagram that if spot is below 1.3563 or above 1.3837 at expiry, the payoff is greater than the premium paid and the buyer of the straddle profits. However, if spot is between 1.3563 and 1.3837 at expiry, then the seller profits. This analysis assumes that the trader takes no other action toward hedging her straddle position.

In short, the advantage of prices being quoted using one of the conventional methods described earlier is that they tell you how far spot must move in percentage or pip terms for the option position to break even. The concept of a breakeven provides a starting point for option traders to think about whether options are over- or under-priced.

At this stage, it is sufficient for the reader to think of the breakeven as follows. If the breakeven is small (large) compared with the amount that the trader expects the spot market to move, then she should consider buying (selling) the straddle. However, in later chapters, we see that this idea is too simplistic. The ability of the options trader to delta hedge means that spot may exceed the breakeven and yet the seller of the option profits.

1.4 STRIKE CONVENTIONS

The term *at-the-money* is commonly used in three contexts in FX options. They are at-the-money spot (ATMS), at-the-money forward (ATMF) and at-the-money (ATM). I discuss each of these below.

ATMS I discussed ATMS earlier. To recapitulate, this is when the strike K is equal to the rate at which the underlying currency's spot market is trading, which I denote by S_t. That is, $K = S_t$ for an ATMS option.

ATMF An ATMF option is when the strike K is equal to the rate at which the underlying currency pair's forward is trading. I assume zero interest rates for both currencies in the first part of this book. Readers already familiar with the basics of forwards will note that this means that the spot and the forward are equal to each other. Therefore, unless otherwise specified, there is no distinction between ATMF and ATMS options until Chapter 9.

ATM Finally, there are at-the-money (ATM) options. Readers already working with options will commonly hear the term *ATM* because this is the most commonly traded and liquid contract in the OTC market. We have not yet built the background knowledge to understand the ATM contract. To do so requires an understanding of implied volatility, the topic of the next section. I therefore explain the ATM contract later in the chapter, but at this stage the reader should think of an ATM contract in a similar way to the ATMS contract.

1.5   WHAT IS VOLATILITY?

Until now we have understood volatility only conceptually as the uncertainty associated with the future price of the spot rate. High volatility implies that the spot rate may change by a large amount and vice versa for low volatility. Here, I make the concept of volatility more precise.

Let us overlay the payoff profile of the straddle with a probability density function (PDF) of EUR-USD.[3] This is shown in Figure 1.6. The standard deviation of the PDF, denoted by σ, is closely related to the probability that EUR-USD moves away from 1.37. Clearly, this probability is higher if σ is larger. Options traders usually annualize σ and then refer to it as *volatility* (more on how to annualize later).

There are two types of σ that are most commonly used for options trading, *implied volatility*, $\sigma_{implied}$, and *realized volatility*, $\sigma_{realized}$. Let us discuss each of these in turn.

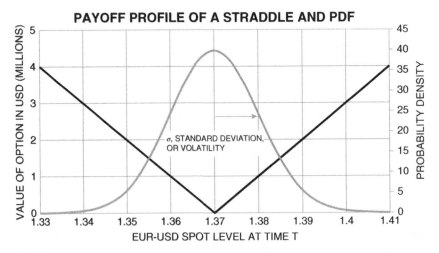

FIGURE 1.6   The figure shows the payoff of a straddle option strategy and the PDF of EUR-USD overlayed. The larger σ, the more chance that EUR-USD moves far from 1.37 and the higher the payoff of the straddle.

---

[3]Readers unfamiliar with the concept of a PDF may consult Section A.1 of the appendix.

1.5.1   Implied Volatility, $\sigma_{implied}$

Suppose an FX option is trading in the market at certain cash price. $\sigma_{implied}$ is the number that one must plug into the Black-Scholes-Merton (BSM) option pricing function, along with several other parameters, in order to match this price. The reader may be confused as to why $\sigma_{implied}$ is a useful concept. After all, one can create an arbitrary function $f(x)$ of a parameter x that is completely different to the BSM function and then back out x such that $f(x)$ matches an option price! x would not represent any economic meaning. The reason that $\sigma_{implied}$ remains interesting is because BSM derived their formula using a plausible description for the PDF of the exchange rate. If the BSM PDF had turned out to describe observed exchange rate movements, then $\sigma_{implied}$ would be a useful quantity with economic meaning; it would be the market's forecast of the volatility that will occur in the future.

Although it does not capture several important features of real markets, fortunately the BSM approach does capture many of them. Therefore, options traders nevertheless think of $\sigma_{implied}$ as an approximation of the market's forecast of the volatility that will occur in the future and as the width or standard deviation of the PDF of spot that is inferred from the prices of options.[4] I continue for the rest of this chapter on this basis. It should be intuitive that the larger $\sigma_{implied}$, the higher the price of the straddle.

The value of $\sigma_{implied}$ changes many times in a typical trading day, but for the purpose of this discussion, let us suppose that $\sigma_{implied} = 10\%$ and the option expires in 1 year. Economically, this means that to a good approximation, over the year, option prices imply that there is a 68% probability that the return of spot is between -10% and $+10\%$. That is, $\sigma_{implied}$ is the *one standard deviation* spot return. The (optional) feature box explains this calculation in more detail. Appendix A.1.3 provides a refresher on standard results relating to normal distributions.

---

[4]Readers familiar with the concept of risk premiums will note that $\sigma_{implied}$ contains a so-called *volatility risk premium* and it is therefore not the standard deviation of the objective PDF but the risk-neutral, or risk-adjusted PDF. I assume risk-neutral investors at this stage in order to build intuition and refer readers to Cochrane (2005) for a detailed treatment of risk premia. Readers familiar with *smile* will also note that the standard deviation must be calculated via volatility swap prices, not $\sigma_{implied}$. Again, I sacrifice accuracy for intuition.

THE BLACK-SCHOLES-MERTON APPROACH

In their seminal work, Black & Scholes (1973) and Merton (1973) priced options by assuming that the log spot return, rather than the absolute return, of the underlying security is normal (see Appendix A.1.3 for more on log-normal returns). I describe the BSM model in detail in Chapter 9 but, in short, their assumption is that,

$$r_t^T \equiv \ln \frac{S_T}{S_t} \sim \mathcal{N}\left(-\frac{1}{2}\sigma^2\tau, \sigma^2\tau\right).$$

Here, r_t^T is the log return between the present time t and T, the remaining time until expiry is $\tau = T - t$, and $\mathcal{N}(\mu, \sigma^2)$ denotes a normal or Gaussian distribution with mean μ and variance σ^2. For simplicity I have assumed zero interest rates at this stage.

For readers unfamiliar with log returns the important point is to note that they are much like standard returns when returns are small. For example, if $S_t = 1.00$ and $S_T = 1.01$, then the return $S_T/S_t - 1 = 1\%$, and $\ln(S_T/S_t) \approx 1\%$. When returns become large, the log return and standard return diverge Among others, one of the advantages of the log-normal approach is that it ensures that the underlying price of the currency can never become negative.

Applying standard results relating to normal distributions, we see that

$$\text{Prob}\left(-\sigma\sqrt{\tau} - \frac{1}{2}\sigma^2\tau < \ln\frac{S_T}{S_t} < \sigma\sqrt{\tau} - \frac{1}{2}\sigma^2\tau\right) = 0.68 \qquad (1.1)$$

Finally, substituting $\sigma = \sigma_{implied} = 10\%$ and $\tau = 1$ year we find that there is a 68% probability that $\ln\frac{S_T}{S_t}$ is less than 9.5% and greater than -10.5%. Therefore, there is a 68% probability that the actual spot return, $\frac{S_T}{S_t} - 1$, over 1 year is between -10% and 10%, because $\exp(-0.105) - 1 = -10\%$ and $\exp(0.095) - 1 = 10\%$.

So far we have considered a 1-year time horizon. Suppose instead that we are interested in a 3-month option. In this case, apply $\tau = \frac{1}{4}$ and $\sigma_{implied} = 10\%$ into the equation above to find that options have priced a 68% probability that spot will be within ±5% of its present value.

An important point to note is that $\sigma_{implied}$ is an annualized number. The one standard deviation return priced into options depends on $\sigma_{implied}$ appropriately scaled by the tenor of the option under consideration.

Another important point to note is that there is typically a different $\sigma_{implied}$ for options of different tenors. So, for example, it is feasible for $\sigma_{implied}$ to be 8% for a 3-month option, and to be 10% for a 1-year option. The variation in $\sigma_{implied}$ as a function of tenor is known as *term structure*. I discuss term structure in detail in Chapter 6. There I change to the more appropriate notation of $\sigma_{implied}(T)$ to denote the $\sigma_{implied}$ belonging to a particular expiry date T.

Therefore, as a heuristic, if the trader thinks that the probability that spot will move by more than ±10% over the next year is greater than 32%, she should consider buying the option and going long volatility. If she has the opposite view, then she should consider selling the option.

ATM Options If interest rates are zero, then an ATM option has strike

$$K = S_t e^{\frac{1}{2}\sigma_{implied}^2 \tau}, \tag{1.2}$$

where $\tau \equiv T - t$ is the time remaining until expiry of the option. The main point to note at this stage is that for typical FX market parameters, $K \approx S_t$. For example, for a 1-year expiry option and $\sigma_{implied} = 10\%$, $K = 1.005 \times S_t$. The difference is smaller for shorter-dated expiries. Therefore, an ATM option looks much like an ATMS option.

This equation comes from the BSM formula, which I discuss in detail in Chapter 10. However, for curious readers, it is the strike K such that the delta of a straddle of strike K is zero, according to the BSM function. It is therefore also known as the delta-neutral straddle (DNS) strike.

Implied Volatility and Breakevens An options trader may prefer to think about $\sigma_{implied}$ in terms of the breakeven that it implies for an ATM straddle, rather than thinking in terms of PDFs. In this subsection, I introduce a simple, approximate rule of thumb to allow option traders to convert between $\sigma_{implied}$ and straddle breakevens.

The breakeven points can be approximately calculated using the following formula,

$$\text{Breakeven(s)} = \text{Spot} \times \left(1 \pm \frac{4.2 \times \sigma_{implied} \times \sqrt{n}}{100} \right), \qquad (1.3)$$

where n is the number of calendar days until the option expires. For example, suppose that $\sigma_{implied} = 10\%$ and the option expires tomorrow, $n = 1$. Then the breakeven is $\pm 0.42\%$ of the current spot rate. Similarly, for a 1-year option, $n = 365$, priced with $\sigma_{implied} = 10\%$, the breakeven is $\pm 8.02\%$ of the current spot rate. Recall from the example in Section 1.3 that the breakeven is also the price of the straddle struck at the current spot rate. The previous formula can therefore be used to calculate option prices.

In practical options trading, three of the most informative (and liquid) options contracts are the overnight, 1-month, and 1-year expiries. To facilitate fast analysis and decision making, it may be worthwhile committing to memory that the breakevens for each of these contracts based on Equation (1.3) are approximately $\pm 4.2\sigma_{implied}$, $\pm 23\sigma_{implied}$, and $\pm 80\sigma_{implied}$ basis points from the current spot level, respectively.

The trader can apply the same rule, but replace the 4.2 with 2.1 if she wishes to consider the breakeven of holding the call option (or put option) alone, rather than the straddle. For example, if $\sigma_{implied}$ for the ATM call (put) option that expires in one day is 10%, the trader requires spot to appreciate (depreciate) by approximately 0.21% in order to break even.

The above rule provides a quick and easy method to convert between $\sigma_{implied}$ and breakevens. However, there are at least two important caveats to note. First, I have ignored the effects of interest rates and *forward carry*. I return to this in Chapter 10. Second, I do not wish to suggest that if the trader's view is that spot will move by more than the breakeven, then she should purchase the option. We shall see in this chapter and in later chapters that because of the possibility of delta hedging, it is the difference between the $\sigma_{implied}$ and $\sigma_{realized}$ that determines the value associated with holding the straddle position and not simply the size of the movement in spot.

At this stage I ask the reader to take Equation (1.3) as given. It may not look like it to readers with prior exposure to options theory, but it is a special case of the BSM function applied to the ATM straddle with interest rates set to zero. The many terms in the BSM function have been subsumed into the number 4.2. I derive this equation using a simple normal approximation in Chapter 3 and then formally in Chapter 10.

1.5.2 Probabilities and Breakevens

In addition to the breakeven formula in Equation (1.3), another useful quantity to note to aid decision making is the probability that the payoff of an ATM straddle exceeds its breakeven. This turns out to be approximately 42%. That is, the shaded area in Figure 1.7 is approximately 42%. This quantity turns out to be close to independent of both $\sigma_{implied}$ and expiry.

I derive this result in the context of the normal distribution in Chapter 6 and in the context of the BSM model in Chapter 9. If the trader's view is that the probability that the spot return exceeds the breakeven is greater than 42%, then she may consider buying the straddle. Else, she may consider selling it.

1.5.3 Implied Volatility and Realized Volatility

In addition to directly considering the probability that spot moves by more than $\pm\sigma_{implied}$ or the probability that spot moves beyond the breakeven point, there are many additional metrics that option traders can use to form

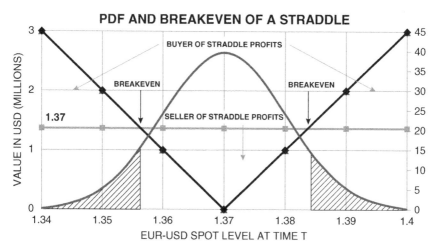

FIGURE 1.7 The figure shows the payoff of the straddle (black), the breakeven points (gray), and the PDF of the EUR-USD spot rate (dark gray). The shaded area is 42%, meaning that the probability that the option payoff exceeds its breakeven is 42%.

a view on $\sigma_{implied}$. One may apply a volatility forecasting model or make a subjective judgment based on an assessment of the present macroeconomic backdrop combined with intuition gained from past experience, among other techniques. However, almost every option trader will study $\sigma_{realized}$ and use it to form at least part of their analysis. This is the topic of the next subsection.

The key point to take away from this subsection is that $\sigma_{implied}$ is a forward-looking metric. It is, to a good approximation, the option market's guess at the width of the future spot PDF and it therefore determines the price that the buyer of the option must pay.

1.5.4 Realized Volatility, $\sigma_{realized}$

Next, there is *realized volatility*, which I denote by $\sigma_{realized}$. Unlike $\sigma_{implied}$, $\sigma_{realized}$ is a backward-looking metric. Crudely put, it is a measure of how much spot has been moving over a particular time period in the past; it measures the standard deviation of the PDF of spot that has been realized. One can see this from a common formula that is used to calculate $\sigma_{realized}$,

$$\sigma^2_{realized} = \frac{\alpha}{k} \sum_{i=1}^{k} (r_i^{i+1})^2 = \frac{\alpha}{k} \sum_{i=1}^{k} \left(\ln \frac{S_{i+1}}{S_i} \right)^2. \tag{1.4}$$

Here, $r_i^{i+1} \equiv \ln \frac{S_{i+1}}{S_i}$ is the log return of spot over a discrete period of time. In practice, this ranges from 5 minutes through to 1 day. There is no market standard sampling frequency and the *best* frequency to use remains an open topic for debate.[5] k is the number of discrete returns in the sample and α is a normalization factor. α is chosen to make sure that $\sigma_{realized}$ is directly comparable to $\sigma_{implied}$.

Recall that $\sigma_{implied}$ is an annualized quantity. Therefore, for example, if one were to use hourly log returns, then $\alpha = 8760$, the number of hours in a year. If instead one were to use daily log returns, then $\alpha = 365$.

Since $\sigma_{realized}$ is related to the average of squared returns, it does not matter if the spot rate has moved higher or lower. All that matters is the size of the returns.

---

[5]For interested readers, Zhang, Mykland, and Ait-Sahalia (2005) provide discussion and suggestions relating to sampling frequencies and methods.

The feature boxes that follow provide some simple realized volatility example calculations and rules of thumb. Here, I focus on the practical issues of how this number is used, and why it is important.

Applying Realized Volatility Perhaps the best way to understand how an option trader may use the calculated value of $\sigma_{realized}$ in practice is via an example. Suppose that the trader is considering purchasing a 1-year expiry option. She may begin by considering the 365 daily log returns over the past year and inserting them into Equation (1.4). Note that the returns over the weekend may be zero and so there are likely to be closer to 260 non-zero returns. Suppose that the outcome of the calculation is $\sigma_{realized} = 11\%$. This tells her that her best estimate of the standard deviation of the PDF of spot returns over the period of time under study is 11%. Suppose next that $\sigma_{implied}$ corresponding to the 1-year option is 10%. The trader must now make a judgment. If she believes that the next year will look somewhat like the previous year, or that the forthcoming macroeconomic conditions appear even more volatile, then she should purchase the option. The expected profit from doing so is approximately 1% multiplied by the so-called *Vega* of the option (see Chapter 5). Alternatively, if the trader believes that the volatility will diminish over the year to below 10%, then she may consider selling the option. Making this judgment is arguably the greatest challenge in successful options trading.

OPTIONS TRADERS' RULES OF THUMB

- For an option with n days until expiry, the market implies that there is a 68% probability that spot is within $\pm \sigma_{implied} \sqrt{\frac{n}{365}}\%$ in n days.
- Therefore, for a 1-year option, the market implies that there is a 68% probability that spot is within $\pm \sigma_{implied}\%$ of its present price in 1 year.

This can be understood via Equation (1.1). Often in FX markets, $\sigma_{implied}$ is a number of the order of 10% and the most liquidly traded options have τ of the order of 1 year (or less). Therefore, again setting

(Continued)

$\sigma = \sigma_{implied}$, $\sigma\sqrt{\tau} \gg \frac{1}{2}\sigma^2\tau$. Also, to first order, $\ln\frac{S_T}{S_t} = \frac{S_T}{S_t} - 1$. Approximately at least, (1.1) reduces to

$$\text{Prob}\left(-\sigma_{implied}\sqrt{\tau} < \frac{S_T}{S_t} - 1 < \sigma_{implied}\sqrt{\tau}\right) = 0.68.$$

We see that, for a given $\sigma_{implied}$, the standard deviation of the spot return scales with the square root of time. We will see that this idea pops up frequently in options theory, particularly when we study the concept of option *Vega* in later chapters.

Our next set of rules of thumb relate to option breakevens.

- For an ATM straddle with n days until expiry, the amount that spot must move in basis points for the position to break even is $4.2\sqrt{n}\sigma_{implied}$. This equates to $4.2\sigma_{implied}$ for an option that expires tomorrow, $23\sigma_{implied}$ for an option that expires in 30 days, and $80.25\sigma_{implied}$ for an option that expires in 1 year.

- Using this formula, traders can easily convert $\sigma_{implied}$ into breakevens.

There are several other important considerations that the trader should make relating to *smile* or *surface*, to the standard error of the estimate $\sigma_{realized}$, and to the volatility of interest rates (or forwards) that we shall return to in later chapters. However, the difference between $\sigma_{realized}$ over the life of the option trade and $\sigma_{implied}$ that determined the initial price of the option provides a measure of the profits that could have been earned from the option position.

REALIZED VOLATILITY

Suppose that the (log) return of spot is $\pm1\%$ each weekday. At weekends it is stationary. Since we are taking daily data, α is set to 365. Let's assume that we have approximately 6 months' worth of data ($N = 182$ data points). Of these, 130 will be $\pm1\%$ and 52 will be zeros, because they occur on weekends. Substituting these numbers into Equation (1.4) we see that

$$\sigma_{realized} = \sqrt{\frac{365}{182}} * 130 * 1\%^2 \approx 16\%.$$

The rule of thumb that option traders should recall is then simply that a daily 1% move in spot corresponds to an annualized volatility of 16%. Similarly, if spot (log) returns 0.5% per day, then its annualized volatility is 8% and so on. So, for example, if the trader's view is that spot will return 0.5% every business day for, say, the next 3 months, and $\sigma_{implied}$ for the 3-month option is 7%, then the trader should purchase the option because she thinks that the option is worth 8%.

1.6   TRADER'S SUMMARY

- Options are bets on volatility. The straddle owner does not care which way spot moves because her payoff is symmetric. She simply requires spot to move a long way, in order to receive a higher payoff.
- ATMS call options and put options can be converted into straddles by adding a delta hedge. This shows that calls and puts are bets on volatility.
- Implied volatility, $\sigma_{implied}$, is a forward-looking metric. It is approximately the standard deviation of the PDF of spot that is priced into options. It is approximately the amount of realized volatility that is predicted by options traders to take place in the future.
- Realized volatility, $\sigma_{realized}$, determines the amount of volatility that actually takes place over a given period of time. Loosely put, if $\sigma_{realized}$ is greater than $\sigma_{implied}$ over the life of an option trade, then the owner of the option has had the opportunity to profit. It is also a commonly used backward-looking metric to determine whether the trader should make the decision to buy or sell an option.
- The price of an option as a percentage of the notional or in pips tells us how much the owner of the option requires spot to move to break even (assuming no other trading).
- It is straightforward to convert between $\sigma_{implied}$ and breakeven points using the approximate (special case of the) BSM formula in Equation (1.3).

- Option prices imply that the probability that spot exceeds the breakeven point is 42%. If the trader's view is that the true probability is higher (lower), she may consider buying (selling) the option.

This chapter has provided a whirlwind tour of the basics of options trading. The following chapters gradually make these ideas more precise and introduce the reader to new concepts, such as options *Greeks*, while retaining a model-free setting.

CHAPTER 2

Understanding Options Without a Model

The previous chapter provided a short tour of the main ideas in options theory. This chapter proceeds with less pace and more detail. The main objectives are to understand option pricing functions, the concepts of delta and delta hedging, and how these ideas relate to each other. Most textbooks on options introduce these ideas in the context of the BSM model. However, one of the objectives in this book is to show that the most important concepts in options theory and practical options trading can be understood without a full stochastic financial model.

2.1 VANILLA OPTIONS

A *European* vanilla call option is a contract that gives its holder the right to buy the underlying asset at the *expiry time*, T, for a prespecified price, K, also called the strike price. A *European put option* is the same except that it gives its holder the right to sell, rather than buy, the underlying asset.

In the context of FX, it is important to note that every option is both a call and a put. For example, suppose that our currency pair of interest is EUR-USD and we buy a $T = 1$-month call option on EUR with strike $K = 1.37$ and notional of 100 million EUR. Then, one month from today, at the expiry time (most often 10 a.m. New York time for FX options) we can, if we choose to, buy 100 million EUR at a price of 137 million USD, regardless of the level of EUR-USD at the time. Here we are treating EUR as the underlying asset. Alternatively, we can treat USD as the underlying asset and reword our example as follows. In one month from today, at expiry time T, we can sell 137 million USD in exchange for 100 million EUR. A call option on EUR is also a put option on USD. The contract in this example is best described as a EUR-call, USD-put option.[1]

Market convention or, rather, shorthand is to name options either calls or puts based on the first quoted currency in the currency pair of interest. For example, the contract described earlier would commonly be called a EUR-USD call option with the *call* referring to EUR. The main exception is in currency pairs involving JPY and CHF where there is no fixed convention.

To further obscure the difference between calls and puts, we will soon see that a model-free result, *put–call parity*, means that risk management practice for both calls and puts is almost identical. The implication is that, as a general rule, option risk managers often do not consider whether the option being traded is a call or a put when assessing its risk.

The two most common types of options are *European* and *American*. These do not refer to the location of the option or exchange but instead refer to the timing of exercise. The difference is that an American option can be exercised at any time up until T rather than at T only, like a European option. The analysis in this book refers to European options for two reasons. First, it is straightforward to show that an American option should very rarely be exercised before expiry. The intuition here is that early exercising an option causes the owner to lose future optionality, which has value. I explain this in detail later in this chapter. Second, perhaps because it is so rare for it to be optimal to early exercise an American option, they are very rarely traded in FX markets.

2.1.1 Option Payoffs

Let us return to the example in the previous section. At time T, if EUR is worth more than 1.37 USD, for example, if EUR-USD is 1.39, then the value of our $K = 1.37$ EUR-USD call option is 2 million USD; if we exercise the option and sell the EUR, then we receive $(1.39 - 1.37) * 100$ million $= 2$ million USD. If, instead, EUR is worth less than 1.37 USD, we simply abandon the option for nothing.

We see that the value per unit of a call option at expiry, V_T, is given by

$$V_T = \max(S_T - K, 0), \tag{2.1}$$

---

[1]One can argue that all options and not just FX options are both calls and puts. For example, a call option on the FTSE could be considered a put on GBP.

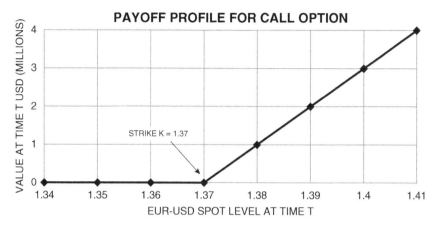

FIGURE 2.1 The figure shows the value at T as a function of S_T of a EUR-USD call option with $K = 1.37$.

where S_T is the spot price of the asset (EUR-USD at 1.39 in our example) at time T. Figure 2.1 plots this function.

In essence, the main task in options theory is to find the value of the option at times $t < T$, or V_t. However, to do so we must make assumptions. Equation (2.1) can be thought of as a boundary condition in that, whatever we come up for V_t for $t < T$, it must converge to V_T as $t \to T$.

2.2   MAKING ASSUMPTIONS

I add assumptions that will allow us to understand more features of V_t. I divide these assumptions into two types: *modeling* and *economic*.

Modeling assumptions relate to the PDF of the spot price. For example, in the well-known BSM model the assumption that S_t follows a geometric Brownian motion and that therefore S_T is log-normally distributed is a modeling assumption.

In contrast, an economic assumption is an assumption about the behavior of market participants. For example, assuming that traders act to maximize profit is an economic assumption. This chapter is devoted to understanding options with (mild) economic assumptions only.

I add modeling assumptions in later chapters. However, I make these assumptions clear with the objective that the reader should be able to assess which assumptions are appropriate to the market conditions at the time of the trade.

2.3 UNDERSTANDING V_t WITH ECONOMIC ASSUMPTIONS

It turns out that we can get quite far in our understanding of options before introducing a full set of modeling assumptions. Indeed, options were traded and successfully risk managed long prior to the seminal formal option modeling contributions of Black & Scholes (1973) and Merton (1973).

At time t we do not know what V_T will be. However, we can form an expectation of its value conditional on the information that we have at the current time t. Let us denote the conditional expectation by $\mathbb{E}_t$ (see Appendix A for a refresher on calculating expectations). I propose that

$$V_t = \mathbb{E}_t[V_T] = \mathbb{E}_t[\max(S_T - K, 0)] \qquad (2.2)$$

is a good starting assumption for the option value.[2] For simplicity, at this stage, the above equation ignores the time value of money. If S_T represents the price of EUR-USD, then I assume that the interest rate on EUR and the interest rate on USD are fixed at zero. In words, the equation above says that the price of the option today is equal to the market's expectation of the payoff of the option at time T. The reasoning is as follows.

Suppose that we instead assumed that

$$V_t > \mathbb{E}_t[\max(S_T - K, 0)]. \qquad (2.3)$$

If this were true, then the buyer of the option would pay a premium of V_t to buy the option, but this would be more than they *expect* to receive at expiry. If we make the economic assumption that traders do not wish to buy assets that they expect to lose money on, then Equation (2.3) cannot be true. Similarly, if

$$V_t < \mathbb{E}_t[\max(S_T - K, 0)], \qquad (2.4)$$

then the seller of the option will be selling the option for less than they expect to pay the buyer at expiry. Assuming that the seller does not wish to

---

[2]Readers already familiar with asset pricing theory or dynamic replication arguments may object that the expectation is calculated under the risk-neutral and not the objective probability measure. However, to focus on practical trading intuition, I assume risk-neutral investors here. I describe the BSM dynamic replication argument in Chapter 9 and refer readers to Cochrane (2005) for a full treatment of risk premia in options and other assets.

trade assets that they expect to lose money on, then Equation (2.4) cannot be true. In the context of these assumptions, after the market has cleared, Equation (2.2) must hold for the option price.

RISK NEUTRALITY AND RISK PREMIUMS

Equation (2.2) assumes *risk neutrality*—that assets are priced such that their price today equals their expected future payoff. In reality, individuals are not risk neutral but are *risk averse*. A risk-averse investor may indeed happily trade assets that are expected to lose. Home insurance is one example. Put options on the S&P500 are another. Profitability in the home insurance industry suggests that the price paid by consumers does not reflect the actuarial probability of a claim so that on average, the buyer loses. However, consumers continue to choose to pay insurance premiums over the actuarially fair price to hedge themselves for when things do go wrong. Modern financial economic theory and, indeed, option pricing theory carefully account for this effect, naming it the *risk premium*. I refer interested readers to Cochrane (2005). However, almost all of the intuition relating to day-to-day option risk management can be extracted from Equation (2.2) and for this reason, I use it in this book.

V_t may depend on any number of variables. At this stage we do not know which variables are important. Some guesses are the level of spot at the current time, S_t, time to expiration, $\tau = T - t$, historical levels of spot $S_{t-1}, \ldots S_{t-n}$ for $n \geq 1$, the price of beer, the volatility of returns, the return on the market portfolio, or anything else that one may be able to think of. Our first inquiry will be into the dependence of V_t on S_t. This dependence is known as *delta*. I discuss other variables in later chapters.

2.4 DELTA AND DELTA HEDGING

If the value of the trader's option position gains (loses) value when S_t rises, and loses (gains) value when S_t falls, then she can mitigate this risk by selling (buying) an appropriate amount of spot. Delta tells us how the option price V_t changes with respect to the first of the variables listed above, S_t, while assuming that all the other variables of interest remain unchanged. The trader uses delta to calculate the correct amount of spot to buy or sell in the market such that her portfolio becomes insensitive to small moves in the spot price.

Recall from Section 1.2 that delta hedging an ATMS call option by selling 50% of the notional of option in the spot market converts the position into a straddle. That is, using a delta of 50% the trader can convert a bet on the volatility of S_t and S_t rising into a bet on only the volatility of S_t. Over the remainder of this chapter we study how to calculate the delta of any option, not just that of an ATMS option in order to convert any option into a bet on volatility only, at least for small changes in S_t.

2.5   THE VALUE FUNCTION

Let us begin by writing the price of an option as a function,

$$V_t = V(S_t, t, \sigma_i, \phi). \tag{2.5}$$

This equation says that V_t is given by plugging the value of S_t, t, σ_i, and ϕ into a function V. V is known as the *value function*. At this point, we do not know its form. For now we are able to proceed without this knowledge.

σ_i is an implied volatility parameter. Although I do not study the dependence of $V(S_t, t, \sigma_i, \phi)$ on σ_i in this chapter, we know from the intuition gained in Chapter 1 that the option pricing function depends on future volatility. I therefore make the dependence explicit at this stage.

Note that σ_i and $\sigma_{implied}$ are not the same thing. I explain the distinction in the feature box. It is not necessary for the reader to understand the subtle difference between them in order to understand the main ideas in practical options theory presented over the first six chapters of this text. However, it is necessary for the study of smile in the chapters that follow.

V_t depends on $\tau = T - t$. However, I assume that T is a known quantity and hence I write the dependence on t explicitly.

V_t also depends on K but this also is a known quantity rather than a variable. However, there are points in the text where I wish to describe how the option price behaves for different values of K. In those circumstances I include K in the arguments of V.

THE DISTINCTION BETWEEN σ_i AND $\sigma_{implied}$

σ_i is closely related to but distinct from $\sigma_{implied}$, which I introduced in the previous chapter. $\sigma_{implied}$ is a quantity that is intimately tied to the BSM formula. BSM provided a form for V. Let us call it $V_{BS}(S_t, t, \sigma_{implied})$. Chapter 9 provides the explicit functional form. If an option is trading at price V_t in the market, $\sigma_{implied}$ is defined as the number that one needs to plug into $V_{BS}(S_t, t, \sigma_{implied})$ such that $V_{BS}(S_t, t, \sigma_{implied}) = V_t$.

Loosely, the reader should think of σ_i as the annualized standard deviation of the spot PDF. If the true PDF happened to satisfy the BSM assumption of log-normally distributed returns, then $\sigma_i = \sigma_{implied}$.

I refer to both $\sigma_{implied}$ and σ_i as *implied volatilities* because they are both forward-looking parameters. This separation makes clear that the ideas presented here are separate and more general than the BSM model and the BSM model is a special case.

ϕ represents all the remaining variables and parameters that can possibly exist, such as our guesses above. We shall see later that foreign and domestic interest rates are also members of ϕ, among others.

At this point, I suppress ϕ in the notation because the focus in the first part of this book is on S_t and σ_i. Developing an understanding of the dependence of $V(S_t, t, \sigma_i, \phi)$ on S_t and σ_i is arguably more important in understanding the basics of options trading than the other dependencies and hence I write $V(S_t, t, \sigma_i)$ for now.

2.6   DEFINING DELTA

The idea behind delta hedging is that, if we know the form of $V(S_t, t, \sigma_i)$, then we can calculate delta as its gradient,

$$\Delta_t \equiv \Delta(S_t, t, \sigma_i) = \frac{\partial V(S_t, t, \sigma_i)}{\partial S}. \qquad (2.6)$$

Readers unfamiliar with this notation may refer to the calculus refresher in Appendix B.[3] This can be understood as follows.

If the trader owns one unit of the option position and sells Δ_t units of the underlying spot, then she will be hedged against small changes in S_t. We can see this as follows. Initially, the value of the portfolio, W_t, is

$$W_t = V_t - \Delta_t S_t.$$

At a later time, $t + \delta$, $\delta > 0$, the value is

$$W_{t+\delta} = V_{t+\delta} - \Delta_t S_{t+\delta}.$$

The change in value of the portfolio is

$$W_{t+\delta} - W_t = V_{t+\delta} - V_t - \Delta_t(S_{t+\delta} - S_t)$$
$$= V(S_{t+\delta}, t+\delta) - V(S_{t+\delta}, t) + V(S_{t+\delta}, t) - V(S_t, t) - \Delta_t(S_{t+\delta} - S_t).$$

I assume that σ_i is constant and hence I suppress it in the notation here. When δ is infinitesimally small, the change in value of the portfolio is, by the Taylor theorem,

$$W_{t+\delta} - W_t = \underbrace{V(S_{t+\delta}, t+\delta) - V(S_{t+\delta}, t)}_{\text{1. Exposure to Time Progressing}} + \underbrace{\left(\frac{\partial V(S_t, t, \sigma_i)}{\partial S} - \Delta_t\right)(S_{t+\delta} - S_t)}_{\text{2. Exposure to Spot Moving}} \dots$$

$$\dots + \text{further terms.} \qquad (2.7)$$

The above equation separates the change in value of the portfolio into three components. The first is due to time progressing. Readers with prior exposure to options theory may recognize that this term is related to the Greek *theta*. For now, I ignore this term but study it in detail Chapter 3.

---

[3]To avoid ambiguity, the notation in Equation (2.6) can be understood as $\frac{\partial V(S_t, t, \sigma_i)}{\partial S} \equiv \frac{\partial V(S, t, \sigma_i)}{\partial S}\big|_{S=S_t}$.

The second term expresses the exposure of the portfolio to spot moving. Setting $\Delta_t = \partial V(S_t, t, \sigma_i)/\partial S$ means that this term becomes zero. The result is that the portfolio is no longer sensitive to movements in spot. By holding the long option position and short Δ_t units of the underlying currency, the trader is hedged in that the value of the portfolio W_t is no longer sensitive to the direction in which S_t moves. More precisely, the trader is delta hedged; remember we assumed that σ_i (and ϕ) is unchanged. In reality σ_i varies with time and we have done nothing to mitigate this risk. I return to this issue in Chapters 7 and 8. This risk is subsumed into *further terms*.

The intuition here is that, if the trader owns an option whose value rises with S_t ($\Delta_t = \partial V(S_t, t, \sigma_i)/\partial S$ is positive), then she should sell spot in an amount such that the gains from the option position are offset, or *hedged*, by losses from the spot position. I will soon show that a call option is such an example. Therefore, the owner of the EUR-USD 1.37 call option from Section 2.1 should sell Δ_t EUR-USD in the spot market against this position. Similarly, if spot falls in value, then the losses from the option position are hedged by gains from the spot position. Δ_t simply tells us the correct amount of spot to trade.

In Section 1.2 the owner of 200 million EUR of the ATMS call option sold 100 million EUR to be left with a straddle that was insensitive to the direction in which EUR-USD moves, because its payoffs are symmetric. It is clear from this example that the delta of an ATMS option is equal to 50% of its notional,[4]

$$\frac{\partial V(K, t, \sigma_i)}{\partial S} = 0.5. \qquad (2.8)$$

Note also that Δ_t changes every time S_t changes because it is a function of S_t. We will see ahead that it is between 0 and 1 for a call option, and between 0 and -1 for a put option, depending on the strike. Therefore, every time there is a movement in the market, the trader must buy or sell the underlying spot. This rebalancing every time the market moves is called *gamma trading*. Indeed, the *further terms* in Equation (2.7) also subsume the Greek *gamma*, which I return to in detail in Section 4.1.

---

[4]Strictly speaking, the delta of an ATMS option is close to, but is not exactly 50% because of interest rate, log-normality, and smile effects. I cover all of these topics in later chapters. However, this is a good approximation. It is exact in the case of a symmetric distribution with zero interest rates.

2.7   UNDERSTANDING DELTA

The previous section showed that we need to know the function $V(S_t, t, \sigma_i)$ in order to be able to take its derivative, calculate Δ_t, and be delta hedged. One of the main objectives of derivatives pricing models is to provide these quantities. However, the aim in this section is to say something useful about this quantity without building a fully specified mathematical model.

To begin, I make the same argument that I made for the value of an option in Section 2.3 for S_t, that under the risk neutrality assumption,

$$S_t = \mathbb{E}_t[S_T] \quad \text{for} \quad t < T. \tag{2.9}$$

Equation (2.9) is best read from right to left. It says that the value that we expect spot to have at the expiry time of the option contract T, conditional on the information that we have at the current time t, is equal to its current value S_t. In other words, we know that spot will move because markets are volatile, but that move could be higher or lower with probabilities and magnitudes such that spot is not predictable using any of the information that we have today. A more concise way of saying this is that S_t follows a *martingale*.

As an aside, readers may note that Equations (2.1) and (2.9) are implications of the Efficient Markets Hypothesis (EMH) in the special case of risk neutral investors. Chapter 1 of J. Y. Campbell, Lo & Mackinlay (1997) provides a textbook explanation.

The probability that spot appreciates can equal the probability that it depreciates to satisfy (2.9), but in real markets, this is the exception rather than the norm. For example, if S_t is 100, then we can have $S_T = 90$ with 10% probability and $S_T = 101.11$ with 90% probability and satisfy (2.9). Such a market is said to exhibit skewness because the probability distribution is asymmetric. I deal with skewness and its effects on option pricing in Chapter 7.

With Equation (2.9) in place we are able to make a statement about Δ_t for call and put options. Consider the call option first. If spot were to appreciate, $S_{t+\delta} > S_t$, and all else is equal, then the expectation of the option payoff is higher. The reason is that once spot has appreciated, we do not expect it to depreciate again any more than we expect it to appreciate again. The non-predictability equation, Equation (2.9), must hold at the later time $t + \delta$ as well. With the higher spot rate, $S_{t+\delta}$, in place the expectation of S_T is higher and therefore the expectation of $\max(S_T - K, 0)$, or $V(S_{t+\delta}, t)$ is higher, too. Applying $V(S_{t+\delta}, t) > V(S_t, t)$ and $S_{t+\delta} > S_t$ to Equation (2.6) we

TABLE 2.1 Trader's Rules

Position	Value of Position if Spot Appreciates	Action to Hedge
Long call	Increases	Δ_t is positive. Sell spot.
Short call	Decreases	Δ_t is negative. Buy spot.
Long put	Decreases	Δ_t is negative. Buy spot.
Short put	Increases	Δ_t is positive. Sell spot.

The option trader should commit these rules to memory. They are valid as long as Equation (2.9) holds.

see that Δ_t is positive. Equation (2.12) in the (optional) feature box provides a more formal derivation of this result.

At this stage it is a useful exercise for the reader to run through the logic of the argument above for a put option to satisfy herself that Δ_t is negative. Table 2.1 provides a summary of the Δ_t associated with four options positions.

DELTA IS POSITIVE FOR CALL OPTIONS AND IT ALSO TURNS OUT TO BE THE PROBABILITY OF EXPIRING IN-THE-MONEY

Interested readers may wish to understand how we can show our result that $\Delta_t > 0$ for call options more formally. First, rewrite Equation (2.9) as

$$S_T = S_t + \varepsilon_T, \tag{2.10}$$

where ε_T is an independent random variable with $\mathbb{E}_t[\varepsilon_T] = 0$. Then,

$$\Delta_t = \frac{\partial V(S_t, t)}{\partial S} = \frac{\partial}{\partial S_t} \int_{-\infty}^{\infty} \max(S_t + x - K, 0) f_t(x) dx \tag{2.11}$$

$$= \frac{\partial}{\partial S_t} \int_{K-S_t}^{\infty} (S_t + x - K) f_t(x) dx$$

$$= \int_{K-S_t}^{\infty} f_t(x) dx$$

$$= \text{Prob}_t(\varepsilon_T > K - S_t)$$

$$= \text{Prob}_t(S_T > K) \tag{2.12}$$

(*Continued*)

where $f_t(x)$ is the time t conditional probability density function of ε_T. Δ_t is therefore the time t conditional probability that the option will expire in-the-money (ITM) and a probability cannot be negative, giving us our required result that Δ_t for the call option is positive.

Eagle-eyed readers may argue that Equation (2.10) is unrealistic because it does not rule out a negative value of S_T. To avoid this issue, the BSM model assumes a log-normal distribution, $S_T = S_t e^{-\frac{1}{2}\sigma^2 T + \sigma T \varepsilon}$, where ε is a standard normal random variable. In the BSM model the result (2.12) does not hold exactly, but for typical values of $\sigma_{implied}$ it holds to a (very) good approximation. For example, if $\sigma_{implied} = 8\%$, then Δ_t for a 1-month expiry ATMS call option is 0.504, but $\text{Prob}_t(S_T > K) = 0.495$. Option traders are therefore comfortable applying (2.12) in many parts of practical options trading.

2.8 DELTA AS THE PROBABILITY OF AN IN-THE-MONEY EXPIRY

Equation (2.12) provided the remarkable result that if Equation (2.10) holds, then Δ_t is equal to the probability that the option expires in-the-money (ITM). By ITM, I mean that $S_T > K$ for a call or $S_T < K$ for a put. In this section, I provide a second and perhaps more intuitive way to understand this result. Then, in Section 2.9, I discuss how one may apply this idea in practical option trading.

I begin by introducing the derivative contract that allows traders to most directly trade the probability that $S_T > K$, the *digital* or *binary*. The payoff of the digital is $\mathbf{1}_{S_T > K}$. Here, $\mathbf{1}_{S_T > K}$ is an indicator function that takes the value 1 if $S_T > K$ and 0 otherwise, as shown in Figure 2.2.

The reason that the digital contract allows the trader to directly trade the probability that $S_T > K$ can be understood by applying Equation (2.2) to the digital payoff. Denoting the price of the digital of strike K by D_t we see that

$$D_t = \mathbb{E}_t[\mathbf{1}_{S_T > K}]$$
$$= \text{Prob}_t(S_T > K). \tag{2.13}$$

In words, the price of the digital is exactly the probability that a vanilla call option with strike K expires ITM. The next step is to show that it is possible, in theory at least, to replicate the payoff of the digital using vanilla options.

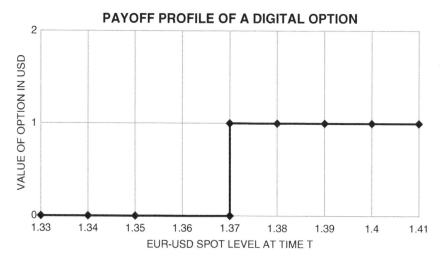

FIGURE 2.2 The figure shows the payoff of a $K = 1.37$ EUR-USD call digital. The horizontal axis shows the level of EUR-USD at the expiry time of the option. The vertical axis shows the payoff to the owner of the option is 1 USD if EUR-USD is above 1.37 at T, and zero otherwise.

Consider the payoff profile that is generated by purchasing a call option of strike $K - \delta$ and selling a call option of strike $K + \delta$, as shown in Figure 2.3. This commonly traded option strategy is called a *call spread*. In the example shown, $K = 1.37$ and $\delta = 0.02$.

The call spread shown in Figure 2.3 has a notional of 100 million EUR. Suppose instead that the notional is set to $1/2\delta$. In this case the payoff would be as shown in Figure 2.4. Already we see that the payoff of the call spread does not appear too dissimilar to that of the digital in that above 1.39 both the digital and the call spread pay 1 USD and below 1.35 they both pay nothing. The payoff is capped at 1 USD and hence I refer to this option strategy as a *unit* call spread.

The price of the unit call spread is

$$\frac{1}{2\delta}(V(S_t, K - \delta, t, \sigma_i) - V(S_t, K + \delta, t, \sigma_i)).$$

Here, I make explicit the dependence of the vanilla call option pricing function V on strike K.

Next, take the limit as δ becomes infinitesimally small. It is clear that as we decrease δ, the payoff converges to the profile shown in Figure 2.2. In the limit as $\delta \to 0$, the payoff of the unit call spread converges to that of the digital.

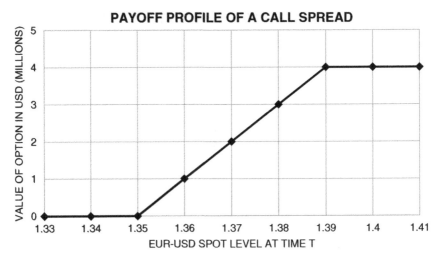

FIGURE 2.3 The figure shows the payoff of a call spread. In this example, it is the purchase of call option with strike 1.35 and sale of a call option with strike 1.39 each with notional of 100 million EUR. The horizontal axis shows the level of EUR-USD at the expiry time of the option. The vertical axis shows the payoff to the owner of the option in USD.

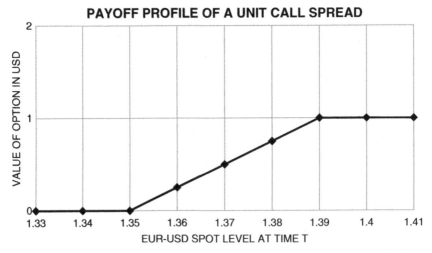

FIGURE 2.4 The figure shows the payoff of a unit call spread. In the example, this is the purchase of call option with strike $1.37 - \delta$ and sale of a call option with strike $1.37 + \delta$ each with notional of $1/2\delta$ EUR. Here, $\delta = 0.02$. Like the digital, the maximum payoff is 1 USD.

OPTION TRADERS OFTEN HEDGE DIGITAL EXPOSURES WITH CALL SPREADS

The idea presented here that one can replicate the digital payoff using an infinitely large notional ($\lim_{\delta \to 0} 1/2\delta$) of an infinitely tight vanilla call spread (buy strike $K - \delta$ and sell $K + \delta$) may appear to the reader as abstract. However, it is not as removed from practical options trading as one may initially suspect. Digitals are commonly traded in FX markets and when hedging the digital directly is not possible (or the cost to doing so is prohibitively large) option risk managers often attempt to hedge their risk from a short digital position by purchasing a vanilla call spread, and vice versa from the long digital.

In EUR-USD, for example, the trader may set $\delta = 0.0025$, or 25 pips. Then, if the trader's position were short the 1.37 strike digital in notional of 1 million USD, she would need to purchase 200 million EUR of the call spread with strikes 1.3675 and 1.3725 in order to hedge. Her payoff would then be as shown in Figure 2.5.

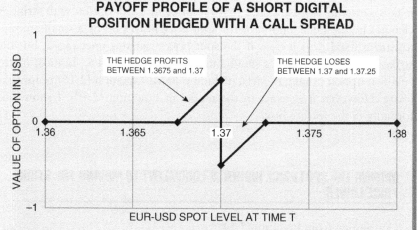

PAYOFF PROFILE OF A SHORT DIGITAL POSITION HEDGED WITH A CALL SPREAD

THE HEDGE PROFITS
BETWEEN 1.3675 and 1.37

THE HEDGE LOSES
BETWEEN 1.37 and 1.37.25

VALUE OF OPTION IN USD

EUR-USD SPOT LEVEL AT TIME T

FIGURE 2.5 The figure shows the payoff profile of a short 1.37 strike digital with notional of 1 million USD and a long position of 200 million EUR of the call spread with strikes 1.3675 and 1.3725. Here, $\delta = 0.0025$ or 25 pips. The call spread is 50 pips wide. The trader's hedge profits in the 1.3675 to 1.37 region and loses in the 1.37 to 1.3725 region. Everywhere else the hedge is perfect.

The price of the digital payoff is given by

$$\lim_{\delta \to 0} \frac{1}{2\delta}(V(S_t, K - \delta, t, \sigma_i) - V(S_t, K + \delta, t, \sigma_i)) = -\frac{\partial V(S_t, K, t, \sigma_i)}{\partial K}, \quad (2.14)$$

from the definition of a (calculus) derivative (see Appendix B). Applying (2.13) we have that

$$-\frac{\partial V(S_t, K, t, \sigma_i)}{\partial K} = \text{Prob}_t(S_T > K). \quad (2.15)$$

Recall that our aim in this subsection is to show that

$$\Delta_t = \frac{\partial V(S_t, K, t, \sigma_i)}{\partial S} = \text{Prob}_t(S_T > K).$$

and therefore the final step is to argue that

$$\frac{\partial V(S_t, K, t, \sigma_i)}{\partial S} = -\frac{\partial V(S_t, K, t, \sigma_i)}{\partial K}. \quad (2.16)$$

to arrive at the required result. Intuitively, the equality in Equation (2.16) makes sense. In words, it says that the price of a call option with strike K changes by the same amount if the spot price moves up by a small amount toward a fixed K as it does if the spot prices remains unchanged, but the strike price is lowered by a small amount toward a fixed S_t. In most mathematical option pricing models, including BSM, Equation (2.16) is approximate. However, it is exact in the model in Equation (2.10). I show this formally in the feature box.

MOVING THE SPOT PRICE HIGHER IS EQUIVALENT TO MOVING THE STRIKE PRICE LOWER

Continuing from Equation 2.11,

$$\frac{\partial V(S_t, K, t, \sigma_i)}{\partial S} = \frac{\partial}{\partial S_t} \int_{-\infty}^{\infty} \max(S_t + x - K, 0) f_t(x) dx$$

$$= -\frac{\partial}{\partial K} \int_{-\infty}^{\infty} \max(S_t + x - K, 0) f_t(x) dx$$

$$= -\frac{\partial V(S_t, K, t, \sigma_i)}{\partial K}. \tag{2.17}$$

The left-hand side is equal to Δ_t and from Equation (2.15), the right-hand side is equal to the probability that the option expires ITM, $S_T > K$.

Since Equation (2.16) is exactly true in models that can be expressed in the form of Equation (2.10), such as the normal distribution, but only approximately true in more commonly used models, such as the BSM log-normal model, I write $\Delta_t \approx \text{Prob}_t(S_T > K)$. Appendix (A.1.3) provides more detail on normal and log-normal distributions.

2.9 APPLYING DELTA AS THE PROBABILITY OF AN ITM EXPIRY IN PRACTICAL TRADING

The insight that we have gained above that Δ_t is approximately the probability that the option being traded expires ITM is particularly useful in practical options trading for at least two reasons.

First, if a trader is able to form a view on the probability that $S_T > K$ through any method, for example, via the statistical analysis of recent returns to construct a PDF, economic research, a combination of these methods, or another approach, then she can calculate the appropriate approximate Δ_t to hold against the option position without having to go through the process of making modeling assumptions and spending computational effort to calculate V_t and then its partial derivative $\frac{\partial V(S_t, t, \sigma_i)}{\partial S}$. For example, if the trader owns the $K = 1.37$ EUR-USD call option with a notional of 100 million EUR and assesses the probability that EUR-USD will be above 1.37 at time T to be 20%, then she should sell 20 million EUR-USD to be delta hedged.

Second, and perhaps more interesting from the point of view of practical options trading, thinking of Δ_t as the time t conditional probability that an option expires ITM can be a fast and intuitive way to (approximately) identify relative value opportunities in options.

When a market participant wishes to trade an option in the OTC market, the market maker, usually an investment bank, provides the price V_t and Δ_t, among other important details relating to the trade. By providing Δ_t the market maker directly provides the probability that the option expires ITM that corresponds to the price being quoted. If this probability is lower than the customer's own assessment, then the customer should consider buying the option, and if this probability is higher than the customer's own assessment, then the customer should consider selling the option. The important point here is that a relative value decision can be made not by using the price V_t but by using an intuitive metric derived from V_t, namely $\Delta_t = \text{Prob}(S_T > K)$.

Astute readers will have noted that there is a caveat here. The Δ_t provided by the market-maker will have been calculated using a mathematical model. In practice, this is likely to be the BSM formula (often with a *smile* adjustment—see Chapters 7 and 8). The calculation therefore depends on some of the assumptions made in the derivation of this formula. If the trader's assessment is that the *true* model of the world would provide a Δ_t corresponding to the same V_t that differs substantially from that provided by the BSM formula, then this method of relative value assessment may not be suitable. In practice, however, many options traders do take this approach as a starting point and rule of thumb to assess relative value among options of different strikes.

2.10 CONSTRUCTING V_t

Sections 2.3 and 2.4 provided four key equations. I restate them here for convenience.

$$V_t = \mathbb{E}_t[\max(S_T - K, 0)],$$
$$S_t = \mathbb{E}_t[S_T],$$
$$\Delta_t = \frac{\partial V(S_t, t, \sigma_i)}{\partial S},$$
$$\Delta_t \approx \text{Prob}_t(S_T > K). \tag{2.18}$$

The objective in this section is to use these equations to understand more about the shape of the option valuation function $V(S_t, t, \sigma_i)$ as a function of S_t, again without resorting to a formal mathematical model. I will show that the answer looks like the gray line in Figure 2.6.

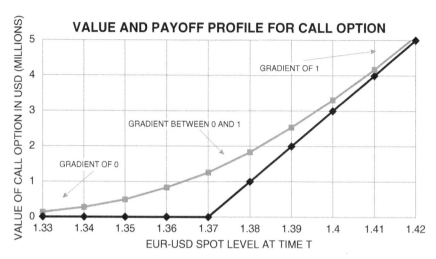

FIGURE 2.6 The gray line shows V_t with $t < T$ as a function of spot for a EUR-USD call option with $K = 1.37$. The black line shows the option's intrinsic value or payoff profile.

Before we begin, let us examine Figure 2.6 in more detail. The black line plots the payoff of the $K = 1.37$ EUR-USD call option. The black line is also commonly referred to as an option's *intrinsic value*. More precisely, an option's intrinsic value at time t is given by $V(S_t, T, \sigma_i) = \max(S_t - K, 0)$; it is the amount that the option will pay out if spot does not change in value between the present time t and the expiry time T, hence it is identical to the payoff function.

The gray line plots the option value $V(S_t, t, \sigma_i)$ as a function of S_t at a time $t < T$. An important point to note is that the gray line is always above the black line for a given level of spot. That is, the value of the option prior to expiry is greater than the value at expiry, $V(S_t, t, \sigma_i) > V(S_t, T)$. The difference between the gray line and the black line is known as the option's *time value*, which I denote by $\Theta_{tv}(S_t, t, \sigma_i)$. That is,

$$\Theta_{tv}(S_t, t, \sigma_i) \equiv V(S_t, t, \sigma_i) - V(S_t, T). \qquad (2.19)$$

The reader should commit Equation (2.19) to memory, although perhaps it is easier to do after rearranging it and verbalizing it: *The total value of an option is given by the sum of two components, its intrinsic value and its time value.*

The reason that the time value is positive can be understood via *Jensen's Inequality*. This is the topic of the next section.

2.10.1 Jensen's Inequality: $V_t = V(S_t, t, \sigma_i) \geq \max(S_t - K, 0)$

Consider a scenario in which S_T can take just two discrete values, $S_T = 1.40$ with probability 0.5 and $S_T = 1.36$ with probability 0.5. Applying our equations above to value the $K = 1.37$ EUR-USD call option that we discussed in Section (1.1) we find that

$$S_t = \mathbb{E}_t[S_T] = 0.5 \times 1.40 + 0.5 \times 1.36 = 1.38,$$
$$V_t = \mathbb{E}_t[\max(S_T - K, 0)] = 0.5 \times (1.40 - 1.37) + 0.5 \times 0 = 1.5 \quad \text{USD},$$

and therefore
$$V_t > \max(S_t - K, 0) = 1.38 - 1.37 = 1.$$

In words, the price of the option with spot at S_t, V_t, is greater than its intrinsic value. This is a simple application of *Jensen's Inequality*.

More generally, Jensen's Inequality states that, for any convex function Φ and random variable X,

$$\mathbb{E}[\Phi(X)] \geq \Phi(\mathbb{E}[X]). \tag{2.20}$$

In our case, the convex function of interest is $\Phi(x) = \max(x - K, 0)$ and random variable is $X = S_T$. Therefore,

$$\mathbb{E}[\max(S_T - K, 0)] \geq \max(\mathbb{E}_t[S_T] - K, 0),$$

or stated more simply,
$$V_t \geq \max(S_t - K, 0),$$

which is our required result. This explains why the gray line is always above the black line in Figure 2.6 and why options have time value.

2.10.2 Trading Intuition Behind Jensen's Inequality

An alternative and perhaps more satisfying way of understanding Jensen's Inequality is through the following trading strategy.

First, suppose that $S_t < K$. Then the intrinsic value is $\max(S_t - K, 0) = 0$. However, since the option has time to run, $t < T$, there is a probability, approximately equal to $\Delta_t \geq 0$, that the option will expire ITM. Since there is a probability of a positive payoff and the payoff of the option cannot be negative, applying Equation (2.2) tells us that $V_t \geq 0$. That is, $V_t \geq \max(S_t - K, 0) = 0$ for $S_t < K$.

The case that $S_t > K$ is more interesting. The intrinsic value is $\max(S_t - K, 0) = S_t - K$. Suppose that $V_t = S_t - K$. The buyer of the option can implement the following. Against the long call option position, sell 1 unit of spot (by borrowing 1 EUR and selling it in the market) and receive S_t USD. By expiry, if spot were to rise to $S_T > S_t$, then the loss from the spot position is $S_t - S_T$, but the option is now valued at $V_T = S_T - K$ and so the gain is $V_T - V_t = S_T - S_t$, exactly offsetting the loss from the spot position. The trader's profit is zero. Similarly, if spot were to fall to a lower value S_T but not so much that it crosses the strike, $S_T > K$, then the gain from the spot position exactly offsets the loss from the option position and the trader's profit is zero again. However, if spot were to fall below K so $S_T < K$, then the gain from the spot position is $S_t - S_T$, but the loss from the option position is just $S_t - K$. The gain from the spot position is bigger than the loss from the option position and the trader has profited.

What has happened here? When spot moved through the strike, the convexity of the option payoff profile meant that the option position stopped losing money even though the *hedge*, the short spot position, continued to make money. It is precisely this convexity that we used in Section 2.10.1 to show that $V_t \geq \max(S_t - K)$.

Here, we have shown that if $V_t = \max(S_t - K, 0)$, then we are able to construct a trading strategy that never loses money, but makes money whenever spot moves through the strike in either direction. Therefore $V_t \geq \max(S_t - K)$ is required to satisfy Equation (2.2) and Jensen's Inequality must hold.

The key point to take away from this section is the following. The fact that an option is worth more than its intrinsic value derives from the probability that spot may move through the strike K. If this probability were zero, then the value of the option would equal its intrinsic value.

2.10.3 American Options

Jensen's Inequality implies that American options should never be early exercised. Exercising an option at time $t < T$ gives its owner the value max($S_t - K, 0$). The owner would do better to sell the option at $V_t >$ max $(S_t - K, 0)$ in the market. There are exceptions to this rule if interest rates are sufficiently large. Here, I have continued to assume that interest rates are zero.

2.10.4 Gradient of V_t

Note in Figure 2.6 that the gradient of V_t, $\frac{\partial V(S_t, t, \sigma_i)}{\partial S}$, tends to 0 when S_t is sufficiently below K and tends to 1 when S_t is sufficiently above K. To understand the reason for this use Equation (2.18) to note that

$$\frac{\partial V(S_t, t, \sigma_i)}{\partial S} \approx \text{Prob}_t(S_T > K)$$

because delta is the gradient of the value function V_t.

Intuitively it is clear that when S_t is very small compared to K, the time t conditional probability that $S_T > K$ is small. Such an option is usually referred to as *deep out-of-the-money* (OTM). Our equation above tells us that the gradient of V_t is small for small S_t relative to K. As S_t increases, this probability also increases. As S_t grows very large compared with K this probability grows to 1. This is illustrated in Figure 2.7.

2.10.5 Drawing V_t

So far we have deduced that

- V_t lies above the payoff function max($S_t - K, 0$).
- The gradient of V_t is close to 0 when S_t is much smaller than K.
- The gradient of V_t increases from 0 toward 1 when S_t increases, reaching approximately 0.5 when $S_t = K$.
- The gradient of V_t is 1 when S_t is much larger than K.

Figure 2.7 illustrates a normal distribution, although this is not necessary. We only required that $\text{Prob}_t(S_T > K)$ grows as S_t rises. This is all of the information that was required to produce the shape of V_t in Figure 2.6.

Although we have established the shape of V_t, we do not yet know several important features, such as its magnitude or equivalently how quickly its gradient moves from 0 to 1. To do so will require a mathematical model, which is the topic of later chapters. However, we will see in the next chapter

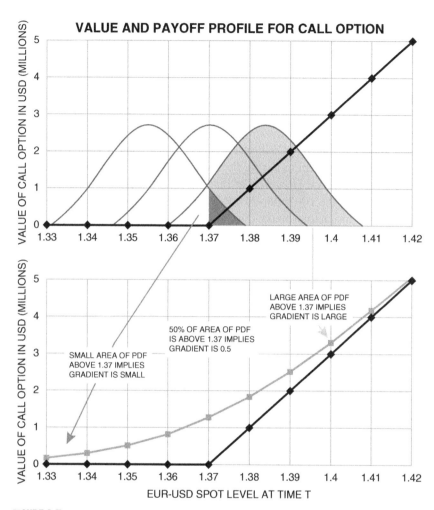

FIGURE 2.7 The upper chart shows the PDF of S_T for three different starting values of S_t. The lower chart maps the area that is under the PDF and also above 1.37 to the gradient of V_t. We see that as S_t increases, the PDF moves to the right, and the gradient of V_t rises, in accordance with Equation (2.12). This area is equal to the delta of the option. Therefore, the delta increases as S_t increases.

that we are still able to use what we have established so far to make more meaningful statements relating to options and practical options trading. We will do so by studying the so-called *Greeks*.

2.11   OPTION DELTAS

Recall that in Section 1.2 the owner of the ATMS call option with notional 200 million EUR sold 100 million EUR in the spot market so that her portfolio became equivalent to a straddle and thereby insensitive to the direction in which spot moves. However, at that point in the text I did not explain how I arrived at the 100 million EUR quantity; I only showed that it works. The ideas in this chapter make this result clear.

If spot is symmetrically distributed as in Figure 2.7, then for an ATMS option ($S_t = K$), 50% of the probability distribution lies above K. The delta is therefore 0.5, or 100 million EUR on an option of notional 200 million EUR. Selling 100 million EUR therefore left the trader *delta hedged*.

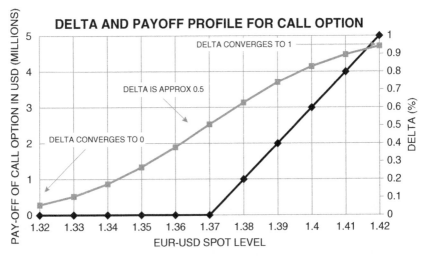

FIGURE 2.8   The gray line shows the delta of the option (right axis) as a function of spot. The black line shows the payoff (left axis). Since the delta is the probability of an ITM expiry, it is clear that the delta must move from 0 to 1. Also, if the probability distribution is symmetric, then the delta must be 0.5 when $S_t = K = 1.37$. However, we do not know the steepness of the slope. Clearly it must depend on volatility and perhaps also on other variables. I return to this in later chapters.

More generally, Figure 2.8 shows how the delta of an option varies with spot. We do not yet know the precise shape of this curve, but we do know that it moves smoothly from 0 through to roughly 0.5 ATMS and then converges to 1 when $S_t \gg K$. The figure provides a good guess at this stage as to how this curve may look.

2.12 A NOTE ON FORWARDS

A forward contract is an agreement to purchase the underlying currency pair at an expiry date T in the future at a strike price K that is agreed upon today. Its payoff is $F_T = S_T - K$. This definition tells us that options are better described as options on forwards, rather than options on spot because an option allows its owner to buy or sell the underlying currency at a future date, if they so choose.

If interest rates are zero, then we can apply Equation (2.9) to calculate the price of the forward contract as $F_t = F(S_t, K) = \mathbb{E}[S_T - K] = S_t - K$.

It is important to distinguish between the price of a forward contract, and the level or price of the forward, f_t. f_t refers to the level of K such that the price of the forward contract is zero. The value of K such that the price of the forward contract is zero is $K = S_t$ and hence the price or level of the forward is equal to the level of spot $f_t = S_t$.

If interest rates are non zero, then the price of the forward turns out to be

$$f_t = S_t e^{(r_d - r_f)\tau},$$

and the price of the forward contract is

$$F_t = F(S_t, K, \tau) = e^{-r_d \tau}(f_t - K). \tag{2.21}$$

Here, r_f is the continuously compounded interest rate in the base currency (EUR in the case of EUR-USD) and the r_d is the continuously compounded interest rate in the numeraire currency (USD in the case of EUR-USD).[5] I derive these results in the next feature box.

---

[5]The notation r_d and r_f comes from financial literature that writes currency pairs as FOR-DOM. For EUR-USD, EUR is the FOR and USD is the DOM.

CALCULATING F_t AND f_t

Consider the following zero-cost trading strategy. Again, I use EUR-USD as an example. First, purchase the EUR-USD forward contract for $F_t = F(S_t, K, \tau)$ USD. Second, hedge by borrowing Δ_f EUR at a rate if r_f, sell the EUR in the market at the prevailing spot rate to receive $\Delta_f S_t$ USD. Finally, borrow an amount X USD such that the strategy costs zero. That is,

$$F(S_t, K, \tau) - \Delta_f S_t - X = 0. \qquad (2.22)$$

At time T the forward contract pays $S_T - K$ USD. The trader must also buy back $\Delta_f e^{r_f \tau}$ EUR at price S_T to pay back the EUR she borrowed. She must also pay back $X e^{r_d \tau}$ USD. The payoff across her portfolio is

$$S_T - K - \Delta_f e^{r_f \tau} S_T - X e^{r_d \tau}.$$

If she chooses to set $\Delta_f = e^{-r_f \tau}$ ex ante, then the payoff is $-K - X e^{r_d \tau}$. This strategy costs zero to implement and carries no risk because the payoff is known at time t. The payoff must therefore be zero to avoid an arbitrage opportunity and therefore $-K - X e^{r_d \tau} = 0$. Solving for X and substituting back into Equation (2.22) gives us

$$F(S_t, K, \tau) = e^{-r_f \tau} S_t - K e^{-r_d \tau}.$$

Finally, f_t is the level of K such that $F(S_t, \tau, K) = 0$. Therefore $f_t = S_t e^{(r_d - r_f)\tau}$ and we can write $F_t = F(S_t, K, \tau) = e^{-r_d \tau}(f_t - K)$.

2.13 PUT–CALL PARITY

Consider the portfolio formed by buying a call option with strike K and selling a put option of with the same strike, as illustrated in Figure 2.9. The payoff of this strategy is $F_T = S_T - K$. Therefore,

$$V^c(S_t, t, \sigma_i, K) - V^p(S_t, t, \sigma_i, K) = F(S_t, K, \tau), \qquad (2.23)$$

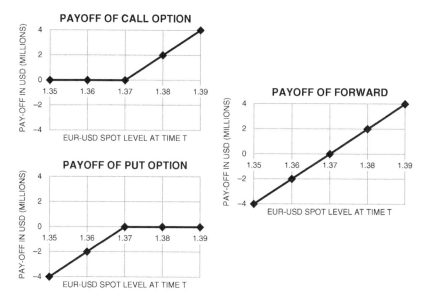

FIGURE 2.9 The upper-left chart shows the payoff of a call option. The lower-left chart shows the payoff of short a put option. The combination of long a call option and short a put option is a forward payoff, as shown on the right.

where $V^c(S_t, K, \sigma_i)$ and $V^p(S_t, K, \sigma_i)$ denote the price of the call and put respectively. There are several important points to note relating to this equation.

First, a put option is a combination of a call option and a forward. That is, one can always sell a forward of strike K to convert a call option of strike K into a put option of strike K.

Second, if interest rates are zero, then using the result from the previous section, we have $V^c(S_t, t, K, \sigma_i) - V^p(S_t, t, K, \sigma_i) = S_t - K$. Therefore, if a trader owns one unit of a call option with strike K, she can sell one unit of spot and borrow K in cash to have a portfolio that is equivalent to owning a put option.

Third, the right-hand side of Equation (2.23) does not depend on σ_i. This is intuitive; the payoff of a forward is linear and so Jensen's Inequality does not apply. This also means that the sensitivity of both the call and the put to σ_i, known as *vega* (see Chapter 5), is identical. This leads to almost identical volatility risk management practice for calls and puts.

Fourth, note that the right-hand side of Equation (2.23) depends linearly on S_t. Therefore, all second derivatives for calls and puts are equal for a given strike. In later chapters we study various second derivatives, namely gamma, vanna, and volgamma and do not need to distinguish between calls and puts.

Finally, if interest rates are zero, then the right-hand side has no time dependency and so calls and puts behave identically with respect to time. The next chapter focuses on this dependency.

The main idea in this section is that put–call parity means that, other than delta or forward risk, the risks associated with holding a call are identical to that of holding a put. Therefore, I do not distinguish between calls and puts over the majority of the rest of the text, and write V rather than V^c or V^p to denote the value function.

2.14   TRADER'S SUMMARY

- The price of an option is given by its expected payoff (see Equation (2.2)).
- The price of an option depends on several variables. Arguably the most important of these is the level of spot, S_t (see Equation (2.5)).
- The dependence of the option price on S_t is given by delta, Δ_t.
- We can show that under certain conditions Δ_t is equal to the probability that the option expires ITM (see Sections 2.7 and 2.8) and we can apply this insight in options trading decision making (Section 2.9).
- The convexity of the option payoff gives rise to time value, $\Theta_{tv}(S_t, t, \sigma_i)$. The value of the option is always greater than its intrinsic value; it is the sum of the intrinsic value and the time value. We can establish this result via Jensen's Inequality (Section 2.10.1) or a trading strategy (Section 2.10.2).
- Applying the idea that Δ_t is the probability of an ITM expiry and that options have time value, we are able to, qualitatively at least, draw the option value function (see Figure 2.7) and the delta profile (see Figure 2.8).
- A forward is the right to buy the underlying currency at T. Options are therefore better described as options on forwards, rather than options on spot.
- Put–call parity tells us that calls are a combination of a put and a forward. Therefore, other than forward risk, puts and calls have identical risk management requirements.

Next, we begin our study of the other important options Greeks, namely *theta* and *gamma*.

CHAPTER **3**

The Basic Greeks: Theta

*T*he *Greeks* are a set of quantities that describe the sensitivity of the price of an option contract to changes in the values of the parameters or variables upon which that contract depends. We already met one of the Greeks in the previous chapter, namely delta Δ_t. There, the variable was the spot level.

More precisely, the Greeks are partial derivatives (in the calculus sense) of the option value with respect to variables such as time, the spot level, and the level of volatility, among others. They are the most important quantities to understand for practical options risk management.

One of the main advantages of thinking in terms of Greeks, rather than thinking about the dynamics of individual options, is that Greeks are additive. Consider Δ_t. If the trader owns n options, each with delta Δ^i, then the amount of spot that the trader must transact in the market to be delta hedged is simply minus the sum of the deltas arising from each individual option, $-\sum_i^n \Delta^i$. The trader's risk management system is able to aggregate the Δ_t^i from each option, leaving the trader with just one net number of concern to manage the Δ_t of her entire portfolio.

Arguably the most important Greeks for practical trading are theta, delta, gamma, and vega.[1] We studied delta in our model-free framework in Chapter 2. However, theta, gamma, and vega can also all be understood before resorting to a formal mathematical model. This chapter focuses on theta.

In short, theta refers to the amount of value that an option loses over a short period of time if S_t and σ_t remain unchanged. In practical trading, this period is usually of the order of one day, or less. Option traders typically maintain high awareness of their theta numbers. If a trader a purchases an option, then her theta will be negative and she is said to be *paying* theta or

---

[1] *Vega* is the name given to one of the *option* Greeks, but it is not a Greek letter.

time decay because the value of an option diminishes as time progresses. If the trader is short an option, then she is said to be *earning* theta or earning time decay. I return to these points in more detail ahead.

3.1   THETA, θ

Section 2.10 introduced the concept of time value $\Theta_{tv}(S_t, t, \sigma_i)$. The main idea was that, for a given level of S_t, the value of an option is greater than its intrinsic value; $V(S_t, t, \sigma_i) > V(S_t, T)$, for $t < T$. Equivalently, for a given level of S_t, the value of an option diminishes over its lifetime. $\Theta_{tv}(S_t, t, \sigma_i)$ and theta, $\theta(S_t, t, \sigma_i)$, are very closely related. Time value is the amount of value that an option loses over its lifetime for a given level of S_t and σ_i, whereas theta is the amount of value that an option loses over a short period of time for a given level of S_t and σ_i. Clearly, the sum of (minus) the theta at every non-overlapping unit of time between the present time and expiry must equal the time value.

In formal mathematical option models, theta is expressed over an instant of time,

$$\theta(S_t, t, \sigma_i) \equiv \frac{\partial V(S_t, t, \sigma_i)}{\partial t}.$$

In practice, traders think of theta as the value that an option loses over a discrete period of time, often of the order of a day. This could be the next 24 hours, between the present time and 10 a.m. New York time the next day when most FX options expire, or another analogous variation. There is no fixed convention across risk management systems. Traders typically refer to this quantity as their *overnight theta*. I provide some examples of overnight theta calculations in the context of ATM options in Section 3.1.1.

The change in option value over a discrete period of time δ for a given level of spot S_t is

$$\Theta(S_t, t, \delta, \sigma_i) \equiv V(S_t, t + \delta, \sigma_i) - V(S_t, t, \sigma_i) = \int_t^{t+\delta} \theta(S_t, s, \sigma_i) ds. \qquad (3.1)$$

This quantity is commonly refered to as an option's *time decay* over period t to $t + \delta$. If the period δ covers the remaining lifetime of the option, $\delta = T - t$, where T is the expiry time, then the time decay is equal to (minus) the time value.

Readers should note the sign convention here, which is to state time value as a positive number and time decay as a negative number. One can almost always avoid ambiguity here by maintaining the logic that option values diminish over time, all else being held constant.

Time value and theta are related as follows,

$$\Theta_{tv}(S_t, t, \sigma_i) \equiv V(S_t, t, \sigma_i) - V(S_t, T) = -\int_t^T \theta(S_t, s, \sigma_i)\mathrm{d}s. \qquad (3.2)$$

In our model-free framework, we can state that $\int \theta(S_t, t, \sigma_i)\mathrm{d}s$ is a negative number because Jensen's Inequality (Section 2.10.1) taught us that options have positive time value. If we assume that θ does not change sign over time, then we can state that $\theta(S_t, t, \sigma_i)$ is negative.

3.1.1 Overnight Theta for an ATM Option

The price of an ATM call option or put option as a percentage of its notional is given approximately by

$$2.1 \times \sigma_{implied} \times \sqrt{n}. \qquad (3.3)$$

Here, n is the number of days until expiry of the option. So, for example, an option that expires in 1 week that has a $\sigma_{implied} = 10\%$ has a price of $2.1 \times 10\% \times \sqrt{7} = 0.55\%$. If the notional of the option is 100 million EUR and EUR-USD is trading at 1.37, then its cash price is 550 thousand EUR, or 753.5 thousand USD. I discuss where this equation comes from in more detail later and ask the reader to take it as given at this stage.

If the spot rate remains unchanged, then one day later, the price of the option is $2.1\sigma_{implied}\sqrt{n-1}$. In our example, the option has 6 days left to expiry, and it is valued at 704 thousand USD. The trader's overnight theta for a 1-week ATM option at $\sigma_{implied} = 10\%$ is therefore 49.5 thousand USD.[2]

More generally, for an ATM call or put option we can write

$$V_t = \frac{2.1}{100}\sigma_{implied}\sqrt{n} \times N, \qquad (3.4)$$

---

[2]The reader may argue that the option is not exactly ATM anymore because even though spot remains unchanged, time has progressed. As discussed in Chapter 1, the difference is small, especially for short-dated options.

where N is the notional of the option.[3] Here, V is in the units of N. If N is measured in USD, for example, then V is also measured in USD. Overnight theta is then given by

$$\Theta(S_t, t, 1\text{ day}, \sigma_i) = V_{t+1\text{ day}} - V_t$$

$$= \frac{2.1}{100}\sigma_{implied}\left(\sqrt{n-1} - \sqrt{n}\right) \times N. \qquad (3.5)$$

Recall Equation (1.3) provided the breakeven of an ATM straddle. Readers will note the similarity between Equations (1.3) and (3.3). To get from (3.3) to (1.3) is straightforward. From (3.3) the cost of purchasing the straddle is $4.2\sigma_{implied}\sqrt{n}$ percent because the trader must purchase both the call and the put. The underlying spot must move by a percentage amount equal to this cost to breakeven; hence Equation (1.3).

Next, let us discuss where Equation (3.3) comes from. It is a special case of the BSM formula applied to an ATM option with zero interest rates. Recall that it is true by definition because $\sigma_{implied}$ is set such that Equation (3.3) matches the market price of the option. However, in the feature box in Section 3.1.3 I assume that spot follows a normal distribution with standard deviation given by σ and show that such a model provides the same valuation equation.

I urge the reader to memorize Equation (3.3). The reason is that market participants usually quote prices in terms of $\sigma_{implied}$. This equation allows a trader to quickly and conveniently calculate approximate option prices and (equivalently) breakevens as well as overnight theta with some mental arithmetic, rather than using option pricing software.

3.1.2   Dependence of $\theta(S_t, t, \sigma_i)$ on S_t

The maximum absolute value of $\theta(S_t, t, \sigma_i)$ occurs when S_t is close to K. Since it is understood that $\theta(S_t, t, \sigma_i)$ is negative, henceforth I refer to the point of maximum absolute $\theta(S_t, t, \sigma_i)$ simply as the maximum or peak $\theta(S_t, t, \sigma_i)$.

In the BSM model with zero interest rates, the peak value of $\theta(S_t, t, \sigma_i)$ occurs when the strike is ATM. That is, $S_t = K\exp\left(-\frac{1}{2}\sigma^2_{implied}\tau\right)$. However,

---

[3]The left-hand side contains a continuous variable t, but the right-hand side contains a discrete variable n, the number of days. The reason that this is consistent is that market convention is for $\sigma_{implied}$ to decrease over the day to reflect intraday time decay as time moves forward. Perhaps more appropriate notation is $\sigma_{implied}(t)$.

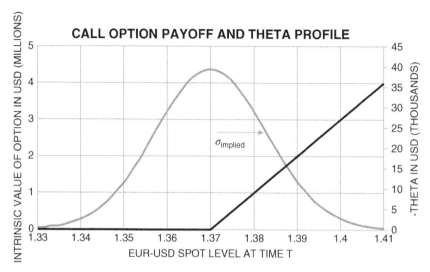

FIGURE 3.1 The figure shows $\theta(S_t, t, \sigma_i)$ for a call option with $K = 1.37$ and notional of 100 million EUR. Here, $\sigma_{implied} = 7\%$ and the option has 1 week to maturity. The peak theta occurs at $S_t \approx 1.37$. At this point, if S_t is at 1.37 in 24 hours, then the owner of the option loses about 39 thousand USD in option value in this example.

as discussed in Chapter 1 this means that $S_t \approx K$ for typical levels of market parameters and for the most liquid expiries (sub 1 year).

Deep ITM and OTM options have much smaller values of $\theta(S_t, t, \sigma_i)$ associated with them than ATMS options. Figure 3.1 illustrates the dependence of $\theta(S_t, t, \sigma_i)$ on S_t.

The idea that the maximum of $\theta(S_t, t, \sigma_i)$ occurs at $S_t \approx K$ is intuitive. Remember, it is the convexity of the payoff that gives options their time value (Section 2.10), and therefore it seems likely that $\theta(S_t, t, \sigma_i)$ will peak at the point of greatest payoff convexity, namely $S_t = K$ and will diminish when S_t is far from K. Let us analyze this in more detail.

Deep OTM Options First, consider a deep OTM call option, $S_t \ll K$. In short, I argue here that since a deep OTM option has very little value to start with, it has little value to lose over its lifetime and therefore $\theta(S_t \ll K, t, \sigma_i)$ is small.

Figure 3.2 shows the PDF and payoff of the situation where $S_t \ll K$. Almost all of the PDF is over the part where the option payoff is zero. There is only a very small implied probability that $S_T > K$ and that the option pays out at all. Even if the option does payout it is likely that the payout is small. Therefore, $V(S_t, t, \sigma_i)$ is close to zero. Since $V(S_t, T) = 0$ when $S_t < K$, we see

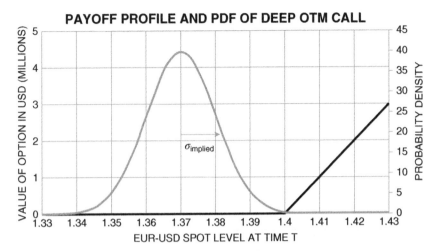

FIGURE 3.2 The figure shows the PDF and payoff profile for a deep OTM option. The probability that the payoff is greater than zero is very small and therefore the option value $V(S_t, t, \sigma_i)$ is small. If S_t remains unchanged, then the option goes from having a low value to zero value. Its $\Theta(S_t, s, \sigma_i)$ must therefore be small for all time points s.

that the left-hand side of Equation (3.2) is close to zero. $\theta(S_t, s, \sigma_i)$ is negative for all time points, s, and so it must be true that $\theta(S_t, s, \sigma_i)$ is also small for all s. If this were not true, then $\Theta_{tv}(S_t, t, \sigma_i) = \int_t^T -\theta(S_t, s, \sigma_i)ds$ would deviate substantially from zero.

Deep ITM Options Next, consider the case of a deep ITM call option, $S_t \gg K$. Figure 3.3 shows the PDF and payoff of this situation. Almost all of the PDF is over the part where the option is ITM. There is only a very small probability that $S_T < K$. In short, I argue here that, since the probability that $S_T < K$ is small, the convexity of the option payoff that gave the option its time value (Section 2.10) becomes largely irrelevant and the value of the option is close to its intrinsic value.

To understand this, recall Jensen's Inequality from Section 2.10.1. First, consider the simple case where S_T can take just two values, $S_T = 1.39$ with probability 0.5 and $S_T = 1.35$ with probability 0.5. Applying our valuation equations from Chapter 2 we find that

$$S_t = \mathbb{E}_t[S_T] = 0.5 \times 1.39 + 0.5 \times 1.35 = 1.37,$$

$$V_t = \mathbb{E}_t[\max(S_T - K, 0)] = 0.5 \times (1.39 - 1.34) + 0.5 \times (1.35 - 1.34) = 3\,\text{USD}.$$

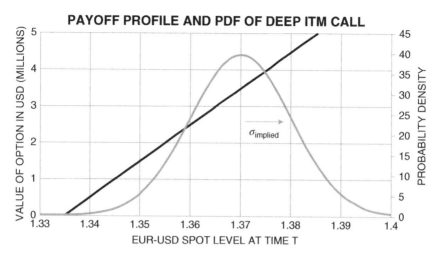

FIGURE 3.3 The figure shows the PDF and payoff profile for a deep ITM option. The PDF lays over the part of the payoff where the option is ITM. The convexity of the option payoff that gave the option its time value becomes less relevant.

Here, I have used strike $K = 1.34$. Since the probability that $S_T < K$ is very small for a deep ITM option, I have assumed that the two possible values of S_T are above K.

We see that $V_t = V(S_t, t, \sigma_i)$ is equal to its intrinsic value $V(S_t, T) = \max(S_t - K, 0)$ of 3 USD. Applying Equation (3.2), we see that the time value of the option is zero and therefore, since $\theta(S_t, s, \sigma_i)$ is negative for all time points s, it must be true that $\theta(S_t, s, \sigma_i)$ is also always zero. The key point that this simple example illustrates is that if there is zero (or small) probability that spot crosses through the strike, then the convexity of the option payoff becomes irrelevant and so $\theta(S_t \gg K, t, \sigma_i)$ is zero or small.

Next, let us understand the same concept using trading intuition in an analogous manner to Section 2.10.2. Suppose that $S_t = 1.37$ and $K = 1.34$, and the probability that $S_T < 1.34$ is small enough to say that it is essentially zero.

Assume that the trader owns the option with notional 100 million EUR and that she sells 100 million EUR spot as her delta hedge. Her payoff is now 3 million USD with almost certainty. The reason is that, if spot stays in the same place, then the option pays out 3 million USD. If spot goes higher, then for every USD the trader makes on the option, she loses the same amount on her delta hedge. If spot goes lower, with every USD she makes on her spot trade, she loses the same amount on her option position. Crucially, and unlike in Section 2.10.2, there is zero probability that spot moves through the strike. She therefore cannot make more than 3 million USD using this strategy.

The important point here is that the above implies that the value of the option is 3 million USD. The value cannot be less because we have shown in the previous paragraph that there is a simple strategy that *locks in* 3 million USD; a rational trader will not sell the position for less. The value cannot be more because, if it were, then the trader could simply short sell the call option for an amount greater than 3 million USD and apply the strategy of being short the option and purchasing 100 million EUR as a delta hedge, and receive a payout of 3 million USD with certainty to generate an arbitrage profit.

The value of the option of 3 million USD is equal to its intrinsic value. Again, as was the case for deep OTM options, the left-hand side of Equation (3.2) is zero and since $\theta(S_t, s, \sigma_i)$ is negative for all time points, s, it must be true that $\theta(S_t, s, \sigma_i)$ is zero for all time points s. The feature box shows this result more formally.

THE THETA OF A DEEP ITM OPTION IS ZERO

More formally, applying Equation (3.2),

$$
\int_t^T \theta(S_t, s, \sigma_i)ds = V(S_t, T) - V(S_t, t, \sigma_i)
$$

$$
= \max(S_t - K, 0) - \mathbb{E}_t[\max(S_T - K, 0)]
$$

$$
= \max(S_t - K, 0) - \int_{-\infty}^{\infty} \max(x - K, 0)f_{S_T}(x)dx
$$

$$
= (S_t - K) - \int_K^{\infty} (x - K)f_{S_T}(x)dx
$$

$$
= (S_t - K) - (\mathbb{E}_t[S_T] - K)
$$

$$
= 0.
$$

Here, I have applied the martingale assumptions from Chapter 2 (Equations (2.2) and (2.9)) and I assume that the probability that $S_T < K$ is zero.

The important point to note is that for both deep OTM and deep ITM options, the fact that the probability that S_t moves through the strike K is zero (or small) means that the convexity of the option payoff is irrelevant and the time value is zero. The reader can work through analogous arguments to those above to show that this is also true for put options.

ATMS Options, $\theta(S_t, t, \sigma_i)$ Is at Its Maximum When $S_t \approx K$ If S_t moves away from K, the time value of an option diminishes. This happens whether S_t moves higher or lower. We already showed earlier that as the option becomes deep ITM or OTM, this time value falls to zero. To establish that $S_t \approx K$ is the maximum of $\theta(S_t, t, \sigma_i)$, our task is to show that this diminishing time value as S_t either moves ITM or OTM occurs in a monotonic manner. The purpose here is to exclude the possibility that as S_t rises (falls), $\theta(S_t, t, \sigma_i)$ increases at some point before falling back to zero as we move deep ITM (OTM). Consider the following two cases.

First, suppose $S_t = K$ initially, and then S_t falls. The intrinsic value started at zero, and remains at zero for all $S_t < K$. However, Figure 3.4 shows that the total value of the option diminishes as S_t falls. Since the total value of an option is the sum of its intrinsic value and time value, it must be that the time value of the option falls as S_t falls.

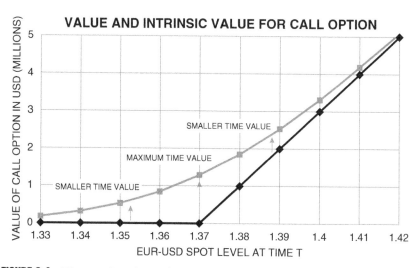

FIGURE 3.4 The gray line shows the option value. The black line shows the intrinsic value. The time value is largest when $S_t \approx K$. In this case, $K = 1.37$. The time value is smaller as S_t moves higher or lower.

Second, suppose $S_t = K$ initially, and then S_t rises. The intrinsic value started at zero, but then gains at a rate of one for one. That is, if S_t moves upward by an amount δ to $S_t + \delta$, then the change in the option's intrinsic value is δ. However, the rise in the total value of the option must be less than δ. The reason is that $\Delta(S_t, t, \sigma_i) < 1$ for all values of S_t. Recall from Chapter 2 that $\Delta(S_t, t, \sigma_i) < 1$ because it is approximately the probability of an ITM expiry and from Figure 2.6 that it is the gradient of the value function. Clearly both of these quantities are less than 1. From the definition of $\Delta(S_t, t, \sigma_i)$, for small δ, the change in value of the option is given by $\Delta(S_t, t, \sigma_i) \times \delta < \delta$. Since the total value of the option rises at a slower rate than the intrinsic value, it must be that the time value falls as S_t rises above K. The next feature box shows these results more formally.

THE TIME VALUE OF A CALL OPTION FALLS AS S_t RISES ABOVE K, OR FALLS BELOW K

The change in intrinsic value due to spot moving from S_t to $S_t + \delta$ is

$$\frac{\partial V(S_t, T)}{\partial S} = \begin{cases} 1, & \text{if } S_t > K, \\ 0, & \text{if } S_t < K. \end{cases}$$

Differentiating Equation (2.19) yields

$$\frac{\partial \Theta_{tv}(S_t, t, \sigma_i)}{\partial S} = \frac{\partial V(S_t, t, \sigma_i)}{\partial S} - \frac{\partial V(S_t, T)}{\partial S}$$

$$= \begin{cases} \Delta(S_t, t, \sigma_i) - 1 & \text{if } S_t > K \\ \Delta(S_t, t, \sigma_i) & \text{if } S_t < K \end{cases} \quad (3.6)$$

$$= \begin{cases} < 0 & \text{if } S_t > K \\ > 0 & \text{if } S_t < K, \end{cases}$$

since $0 < \Delta(S_t, t, \sigma_i) < 1$ (as shown in Chapter 2). Time value therefore increases as S_t moves toward K, peaking at $S_t = K$, and then decreases as S_t becomes greater than K.

So far I have shown that $\Theta_{tv}(S_t, t, \sigma_i)$ falls as S_t falls below K, and that it falls as S_t rises above K. Therefore, the peak in time value must occur when $S_t = K$. However, our task was to show that $\theta(S_t, t, \sigma_i)$ peaks at $S_t = K$, not that $\Theta_{tv}(S_t, t, \sigma_i)$ peaks at $S_t = K$. It is intuitive that the peak in $\Theta_{tv}(S_t, t, \sigma_i)$ occurs close to the same point as the peak in $\theta(S_t, t, \sigma_i)$. After all, these quantities are closely related in that $\Theta(S_t, t, \sigma_i)$ is just the sum (integral) of $\theta(S_t, t, \sigma_i)$ over time. However, we may also obtain the result formally by differentiating Equation (3.6) as shown in the next feature box.

MAGNITUDE OF THETA FOR A CALL OPTION FALLS AS S_t RISES ABOVE K, OR FALLS BELOW K

$$\frac{\partial \theta(S_t, t, \sigma_i)}{\partial S} = \frac{\partial}{\partial S} \frac{\partial \Theta_{tv}(S_t, t, \sigma_i)}{\partial t} = \frac{\partial}{\partial S}\left(\frac{\partial V(S_t, t, \sigma_i)}{\partial t} - \frac{\partial V(S_t, T)}{\partial t}\right)$$

$$= \frac{\partial}{\partial t}\left(\frac{\partial V(S, t, \sigma_i)}{\partial S} - \frac{\partial V(S, T)}{\partial S}\right)$$

$$= \frac{\partial \Delta(S, t, \sigma_i)}{\partial t}$$

$$= \frac{\partial}{\partial t}\text{Prob}_t(S_T > K)$$

$$= \begin{cases} > 0 & \text{if } S_t > K \\ < 0 & \text{if } S_t < K. \end{cases} \quad (3.7)$$

There are four important points to note here. First, I use the approximate result from Section 2.4 that $\Delta(S_t, t, \sigma_i) \approx \text{Prob}_t(S_T > K)$.

Second, I rely on the reader's intuition to understand the approximations in Equation (3.7). The intuition is that an ITM option is more likely to expire ITM if spot remains unchanged and time moves on, and similarly an OTM option is more likely to expire OTM if spot remains unchanged and time moves on because in both cases spot has less time remaining to be able to move through K.

Third, while Equation (3.7) is exact if we assume that S_T follows the model described in Equation (2.10), it may be subtly different in different models. For example, in the BSM model (Chapter 10),

(Continued)

Equation (3.7) becomes

$$\frac{\partial \theta(S,t,\sigma_i)}{\partial S} = \begin{cases} > 0 & \text{if } S_t > K \exp\left(-\frac{1}{2}\sigma^2(T-t)\right) \\ < 0 & \text{if } S_t < K \exp\left(-\frac{1}{2}\sigma^2(T-t)\right). \end{cases}$$

Finally, recall that $\theta(S_t,t,\sigma_i)$ is negative. Equation (3.7) tells us that $\theta(S_t,t,\sigma_i)$ becomes more negative as S_t moves upward from below toward K and then becomes less negative as S_t moves upward away from K, reaching its peak absolute value at $S_t \approx K$. As discussed above, if $\sigma_{implied} = 10\%$ and there is 1 month remaining until expiry, $\exp\left(-\frac{1}{2}\sigma^2(T-t)\right) = 0.9995 \approx 1$. Therefore, even in the BSM model the peak absolute value of $\theta(S_t,t,\sigma_i)$ occurs at $S_t \approx K$ provided the option is short dated (more on this in Section 3.1.3). This is true in almost all models used in practical options trading.

3.1.3 Dependence of $\theta(S_t, t, \sigma_i)$ on t

The theta of an option is smaller for a long-dated expiry option than it is for a short-dated option. For example, if S_t remains unchanged for say, 1 day, then the decay in the value of a 1-year expiry option (becoming a 364-day expiry option) is smaller than the decay on a 1-week expiry option (becoming a 6-day expiry option),

$$\frac{\partial \theta(S_t,t,\sigma_i,T)}{\partial T} > 0. \tag{3.8}$$

That is, $\theta(S_t,t,\sigma_i)$ becomes less negative as we extend the maturity or expiry of the option. I described this effect in Section 3.1.1. There, I claimed that the price of an option grows with $\sqrt{n}$, where n represents the number of days until expiry. Here, I attempt to provide an intuitive justification for this, and also show that this means that theta bills become less of a concern the longer dated the option expiry.

Consider the following simple approach:

$$\ln \frac{S_n}{S_0} = \sum_{i=1}^{n} r_i$$

where $r_i = \ln \frac{S_i}{S_{i-1}}$, n is the number of days until expiry, S_n is the spot value at expiry, and S_0 is the starting spot value. Readers less familiar with the additive nature of log returns may consult the next feature box.

Assuming that the r_i are not autocorrelated and are identically distributed, then taking standard deviations on both sides we have that

$$\sigma\left(\ln \frac{S_n}{S_0}\right) = \sqrt{n}\sigma(r_1). \tag{3.9}$$

I provide some evidence that autocorrelations in daily returns are small in Chapter 11. If σ_i represents the annualized standard deviation, $\sigma\left(\ln \frac{S_{365}}{S_0}\right)$, then the above equation becomes

$$\sigma\left(\ln \frac{S_n}{S_0}\right) = \sqrt{\frac{n}{365}}\sigma_i. \tag{3.10}$$

The important point to note is that the standard deviation of S_n grows with the square root of the number of days n. Therefore, the further that time n is in the future, the more uncertainty there is about the spot price, as we would expect, but the rate of increase of this uncertainty is diminishing in a square root manner.

Consider a 1-year option, $n = 365$ days. The standard deviation of the PDF of $\ln \frac{S_n}{S_0}$ is σ_i. One day later, this standard deviation is $\sigma_i \frac{\sqrt{364}}{\sqrt{365}}$. The change is

$$\delta\sigma(365) \equiv \frac{\sigma_i}{\sqrt{365}}\left(\sqrt{365} - \sqrt{364}\right).$$

Similarly, consider a 1-month option, $n = 30$ days. The change in the width of the PDF over a day is

$$\delta\sigma(30) \equiv \frac{\sigma_i}{\sqrt{365}}\left(\sqrt{30} - \sqrt{29}\right).$$

Clearly $\delta\sigma(30) > \delta\sigma(365)$. The key point is that the standard deviation of the PDF of the spot distribution contracts at a greater rate the shorter time to expiry. Setting $T = n/365$ and so that we can think of time as measured in years rather than days, we have that

$$\frac{\partial\sigma\left(\ln \frac{S_T}{S_0}\right)}{\partial T} = \frac{1}{2\sqrt{T}}\sigma_i,$$

which is larger when T is smaller.

LOG RETURNS

The advantage of using log, rather than simple, returns is that compounding, a multiplicative operation, becomes an additive operation. This can be seen as follows. The simple return from time t to $t + \Delta$ is defined by

$$R_t \equiv \frac{S_t}{S_{t-1}} - 1.$$

The simple return over the previous k periods (from time $t - (k - 1)$ to t) is then

$$1 + R_t^k = (1 + R_t) \cdot (1 + R_{t-1}) \ldots \left(1 + R_{t-(k-1)}\right)$$

$$= \frac{S_t}{S_{t-1}} \cdot \frac{S_{t-1}}{S_{t-2}} \ldots \frac{S_{t-(k-1)}}{S_{t-k}} = \frac{S_t}{S_{t-k}}.$$

The continuously compounded return is

$$r_t^k = \log(1 + R_t^k) = \log\left((1 + R_t) \cdot (1 + R_{t-1}) \ldots \left(1 + R_{t-(k-1)}\right)\right)$$

$$= \log(1 + R_t) + \log(1 + R_{t-1}) + \cdots + \log\left(1 + R_{t-(k-1)}\right)$$

$$= r_t + r_{t-1} + \cdots + r_{t-(k-1)},$$

which is simply the sum of continuously compounded single-period returns. The derivation of the statistical properties of returns over multiple periods is considerably easier for additive rather than multiplicative processes.

To understand how this affects theta, consider Figure 3.5. It shows two PDFs with standard deviations of $\sigma_i \sqrt{T_1}$ and $\sigma_i \sqrt{T_2}$, where $T_2 > T_1$. By inspecting Figure 3.5 and recalling that the price of the option is equal to its expected payoff (Equation (2.2)), the reader can intuit that the price of the option increases with the standard deviation of the PDF. The longer-dated option with standard deviation $\sigma_i \sqrt{T_2}$ has more of the PDF over the area where the option payoff is higher than the shorter-dated option with standard deviation $\sigma_i \sqrt{T_1}$. It is also therefore intuitive that, as 1 day passes, the

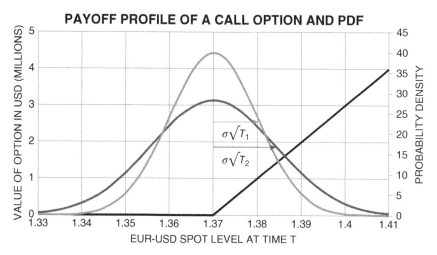

FIGURE 3.5 The figure shows two PDFs, with standard devations of $\sigma_i\sqrt{T_1}$ and $\sigma_i\sqrt{T_2}$, where $T_2 > T_1$. These overlay the payoff of a 1.37 strike call option. The value of the option is larger for the PDF with $\sigma_i\sqrt{T_2}$. The reason is that more of the area under this (wider) PDF is over the area where the payoff of the option is larger.

longer-dated option decays at a slower rate than the shorter-dated option, because the standard deviation contracts by $\delta\sigma(T_2)$, which is smaller than $\delta\sigma(T_1)$.

I make this idea more concrete in the next feature box by showing that the option price is itself linear in σ, at least in the context of a normal PDF.

PRICE OF ATMS UNDER A NORMAL PDF

I provide an approximate derivation of the price of an ATMS option (Equation (3.3)). A full derivation of this equation requires an understanding of the BSM model of Chapter 9 and the log-normal distribution. At this stage, I apply the simpler, normal distribution and appeal to the results from Appendix A.1.3 that show that, under typical market conditions, the normal and log-normal distributions look similar.

(Continued)

I use a normal PDF to model the spot rate with mean μ and standard deviation σ. First, note that $\mu = \mathbb{E}[S_T]$ and recall that $\mathbb{E}[S_T] = S_t = K$ because the option is ATMS. I therefore use $\mu = K$.

Next, recall from Chapter 1 that $\sigma_{implied}$ referred to the annualized standard deviation of the spot rate. Strictly put, this applied to the BSM lognormal PDF. Since I apply a normal PDF here, I denote the annualized standard deviation by $\sigma_i^* S_t$.

Earlier, I showed that the standard deviation grows proportional to $\sqrt{n}$, where n is the number of expiry days. Therefore, I write the n-day standard deviation as $\sigma_n = \sqrt{\frac{n}{365}}\sigma_i^* S_t$.

Finally, I apply Equation (2.2) to calculate the option price:

$$V(S_t, K, t, \sigma_i) = \int_{-\infty}^{\infty} \max(x - K, 0) f_t(x) dx$$

$$= \frac{1}{\sqrt{2\pi\sigma_n^2}} \int_K^{\infty} (x - K) \exp\left(-\frac{(x-K)^2}{2\sigma_n^2}\right) dx$$

$$= \frac{1}{\sqrt{2\pi\sigma_n^2}} \left[-\sigma_n^2 \exp\left(-\frac{(x-K)^2}{2\sigma_n^2}\right)\right]_K^{\infty}$$

$$= \frac{\sigma_n}{\sqrt{2\pi}}$$

$$= \sqrt{\frac{n}{365 \times 2\pi}}\sigma_i^* S_t$$

$$\approx 2.1\,\text{bps} \times \sigma_i^* \times \sqrt{n} \times S_t. \tag{3.11}$$

When n is large, $\sqrt{n} - \sqrt{n-1}$ is smaller than when n is small. Hence, theta bills are smaller for longer expiry options.

Finally, note that the breakeven of the ATMS straddle is therefore

$$4.2\text{ bps} \times \sigma_i^* \times \sqrt{n} \times S_t \tag{3.12}$$

because the trader must purchase both the call and the put.

3.2   TRADER'S SUMMARY

- Theta $\theta(S_t, t, \sigma_i)$ represents the amount of value that an option loses over a short period of time if spot remains unchanged.
- The value of an ATMS call or put option with n days until expiry is approximately $2.1\sigma_{implied}\sqrt{n}$.
- Overnight theta is the amount of value that an option loses in one day. For an ATMS option it can be calculated using Equation (3.5).
- Shorter-dated options lose value at a faster rate than longer-dated options. The reason is that the width of the PDF grows in proportion to $\sqrt{T}$.
- Deep OTM and deep ITM have little theta. The peak absolute value of theta when an option is (approximately) ATMS, $S_t \approx K$.

Theta is closely related to another Greek, *gamma*. In fact, we shall see in Chapter 9 that in the BSM framework one maps to the other via $\sigma_{implied}$. Gamma is the topic of the next chapter.

CHAPTER 4

The Basic Greeks: Gamma

Gamma describes how the delta of an option changes as the spot price moves. In practical option trading, it is commonly scaled to the change in the delta of an option in units of the *base* currency (EUR in the case of EUR-USD or USD in the case of USD-JPY, for example) for a 1% change in the spot rate. A gamma position of +10 million EUR loosely means that if EUR-USD strengthens (weakens) by 1%, then the delta increases (decreases) by 10 million EUR.

The change in delta that results from gamma and a changing spot rate means that the trader must continually trade the underlying currencies in the market in order to remain *delta hedged* and hence insensitive to the direction in which spot moves. For a EUR-USD option, if the gamma position is +10 million EUR, then by the time EUR-USD spot has moved 1% higher, the trader must have sold 10 million EUR in order to be delta hedged.

It is intriguing to note that while a spot trader typically trades when he has a view on the direction in which spot will move next, an option trader who is delta hedging her gamma position trades spot in order *not* to take a view on the next movement of spot! Recall from Section 2.4 that after the trader executes the delta hedge, she is indifferent as to the direction in which spot moves.

Option traders often refer to options that expire in (approximately) one month or less as *gamma contracts*. In Chapter 1, I described how the buyer (seller) of a call or put option is said to be *long (short) volatility*. If a trader's volatility exposure comes from an option with an expiry date of approximately one month or under, then the buyer (seller) of the option is commonly said to be *long (short) gamma*. The reason is that, as we shall see in this chapter, the (local) gamma of an ATMS option increases as the expiry date T decreases.

In all mathematical option pricing models, gamma, theta, and volatility are intimately related to each other. It is important to understand these relationships. Here, I provide intuition, leaving the quantitative relationships to Chapter 10.

4.1 GAMMA, Γ

We already studied delta, Δ_t, in Section 2.4. Gamma, Γ_t, is closely related. It refers to how delta changes with S_t. Formally,

$$\Delta_t = \Delta(S_t, t, \sigma_i) = \frac{\partial V(S_t, t, \sigma_i)}{\partial S} \approx \text{Prob}_t(S_T > K), \tag{4.1}$$

$$\Gamma_t = \Gamma(S_t, t, \sigma_i) = \frac{\partial \Delta(S_t, t, \sigma_i)}{\partial S} = \frac{\partial^2 V(S_t, t, \sigma_i)}{\partial S^2}. \tag{4.2}$$

Note that I continue to apply $\Delta_t \approx \text{Prob}_t(S_T > K)$, which is only exactly true if Equation (2.10) holds and is otherwise approximate in most option pricing models. The framework that we have developed so far tells us that Γ_t is positive for the call option. This can be understood using Figure 2.7. As S_t rises, the probability that $S_T > K$ or, equivalently, $\Delta(S_t, t, \sigma_i)$ rises and so, using the definition above, $\Gamma(S_t, t, \sigma_i)$ is positive. I leave it as an exercise for the reader to show that $\Gamma(S_t, t, \sigma_i)$ is also positive for put options by thinking through how Δ_t for the put changes with S_t, rather than by using the put–call parity relationship.

What does this mean for practical option risk management? Suppose that the trader has purchased the EUR-USD 1.37 strike call option with notional of 100 million EUR, and $S_t = 1.37$. Figure 2.7 tells us that $\Delta(1.37, t, \sigma_i)$ is 0.5. Therefore, in order to be delta hedged, the trader must sell 50 million EUR at 1.37. Recall the reasoning here from Section 2.4.

Suppose that a short period of time δ later, EUR-USD rises and $S_{t+\delta} = 1.39$. The new delta $\Delta(1.39, t + \delta, \sigma_i)$ is larger than 0.5 because the probability of an ITM expiry has increased. Suppose that our judgment (see Section 2.9) or a full mathematical model (see Chapter 10 for BSM) reveals that $\Delta(1.39, t + \delta, \sigma_i)$ is 0.75. The trader had already sold 50 million EUR at 1.37 and so to be delta hedged she must sell an additional 25 million EUR at 1.39 to bring the total position to short 75 million EUR.

Finally, a further period of time δ elapses and EUR-USD falls back again to 1.37. Now, $\Delta(1.37, t + 2\delta, \sigma_i) = 0.5$ and so the trader must purchase 25 million EUR at 1.37 to reduce the short 75 million EUR position to short 50 million EUR.

What is happening here? The trader is *gamma trading*. That is, every time spot rises, the option's delta becomes longer and the trader sells spot. Similarly, each time spot goes down, the option's delta becomes shorter and the trader buys spot.

In our previous specific example, the trader profited from spot trading; she sold 50 million EUR at 1.37, sold 25 million EUR at 1.39, and bought 25 million EUR at 1.37. With spot at 1.37, the value of all these trades is 500 thousand USD. However, this does not imply that the trader has made a profit overall.

It was delta hedging, or gamma trading, the option position that allowed the trader to sell spot high and buy low and generate 500 thousand USD. However, initially establishing this option position cost a premium of V_t and this value is diminishing over time. The trader has paid time decay of $\Theta(S_t, t, 2\delta, \sigma_i) = V(1.37, t + 2\delta, \sigma_i) - V(1.37, t, \sigma_i)$. The question of whether the trader has made or lost money comes down to whether the profits from gamma trading have exceeded the time decay.

Suppose that δ is small. That is, EUR-USD moved from 1.37 to 1.39 and then returned to 1.37 in a very short space of time. Such a fast move can be described as a *volatile* market. In this case, the time decay is smaller than if the same move in EUR-USD occurred over a longer period of time. This makes clear that the owner of the option profits from volatile markets; the trader is able to gamma trade while paying less time decay. The seller of the option benefits from calm markets; the time decay that is earned exceeds the losses of gamma trading.

An important point to note is that option traders price options in anticipation of future volatility. If future volatility (σ_i or $\sigma_{implied}$) is anticipated to be high, then options command a high price and therefore the time decay will also be high. The converse is true if future volatility is anticipated to be low. Therefore, perhaps a better way of phrasing our statement above is that the owner of the option profits when markets are more volatile than had been anticipated and priced into the option. The reader may have noted that we are already moving toward discussions that compare $\sigma_{realized}$ with $\sigma_{implied}$.

4.2 GAMMA AND TIME DECAY

Suppose that in the example of the previous section, the expiry date of the option is 28 days, $\delta = 1$ week, and $\sigma_{implied} = 10\%$. Since the option starts as an ATMS option, and is also an ATMS option after the time period of 2 weeks (2δ), because spot returns to the strike 1.37, we can apply Equation (3.4) to calculate the time decay. The distinction between ATM and ATMS here is too small to be of concern.

$$V(1.37, t + 2\delta, \sigma_i) - V(1.37, t, \sigma_i) = [2.1 \times 10\% \times (\sqrt{14} - \sqrt{28})] \text{ bps} \times N$$

$$= -439 \text{ thousand USD}, \qquad (4.3)$$

where $N = 100$ million EUR $\times 1.37$ to get the notional of the option in USD.

This calculation makes clear that the owner of the option has made money over the period of two weeks. She made 500 thousand USD through her gamma trading effort, and paid 439 thousand USD in time decay, leaving her with a profit of 61 thousand USD.

Recall that in Chapter 1 we discussed $\sigma_{implied}$ as the amount of volatility that is predicted (by options traders) to take place in the future and $\sigma_{realized}$ as the amount of volatility that actually takes place over the lifetime of the option. Having now understood the concept of gamma trading, we can see why the option trader's profits are related to the difference between $\sigma_{implied}$ and $\sigma_{realized}$ over the lifetime of the trade. If $\sigma_{realized}$ is high, then the trader is provided with more opportunity to gamma trade. If $\sigma_{implied}$ is low, then the cost of purchasing the option and therefore the time decay that we calculated in Equation (4.3) is lower.

There are important subtleties relating to gamma and time decay that I study later in the chapter, but the important point for the reader to understand at this stage is the following. Loosely put, option traders face a constant trade-off between gamma and time decay. The owner of the option must ensure that the value of her gamma trading efforts exceeds her time decay.

4.3 TRADERS' GAMMA, Γ_{trader}

The definition of gamma in Equation (4.2) is common in formal mathematical option models. It is the change in delta for an infinitesimally small move in S_t. However, similar to Θ, in practical options trading, gamma is scaled for convenience in some way. I refer to the scaled quantity as trader's gamma Γ_{trader}. Most commonly, gamma is scaled so that Γ_{trader} represents the change in delta that corresponds to a one percentage point (log) return in S_t.

The relationship between Γ and Γ_{trader} is given by

$$\Gamma_{trader}(S_t, t, \sigma_i) = \frac{S_t}{100} \Gamma(S_t, t, \sigma_i). \tag{4.4}$$

To understand this scaling, let us work through a simple example. Suppose that EUR-USD is trading at 1.37 and $\Gamma(1.37, t, \sigma_i) = 1000$ million EUR. If EUR-USD appreciates to 1.3750, then the change in the trader's delta is given by $\Gamma(1.37, t) \times 0.0050 = 5$ million EUR (approximately, assuming negligible higher order effects). Therefore, assuming that at spot 1.37 the trader was delta hedged, she should have sold 5 million EUR by the time spot reached 1.3750 in order to remain delta hedged.

We can get to the same result using the trader's gamma. Applying our equation above, $\Gamma_{trader}(1.37, t, \sigma_i) = 13.7$ million EUR. The (log) return from the spot move is $\ln(1.3750/1.37) = 0.36\%$. Therefore, the change in delta is $\Gamma_{trader} \times 0.36$. Applying our equation above, this is $(1.37/100) \times 1000 \times 0.36 = 5$ million EUR.

The reason that practical trading involves the use of Γ_{trader} rather than Γ is that traders typically find it more convenient to think about percentage changes (or log changes) in spot rather than absolute changes, so that the absolute level of spot plays no part. Given Γ_{trader}, it is then quick and straightforward to calculate the delta hedge that the trader must execute.

4.4 GAMMA–TIME DECAY TRADE-OFFS IN MORE DETAIL

So far I have provided an introduction to the gamma–time decay trade-off. There have been two main ideas. First, profits from the trader's gamma trading offset the time decay. Second, the extent to which they offset depends on $\sigma_{realized}$ compared to $\sigma_{implied}$. Although thinking in this way provides a useful starting point toward understanding gamma and time decay, it ignores important subtleties.

For example, what if spot rises, prompting a gamma trading trader to sell spot, only for spot to rise once more? Then theta is negative as always but so are the "profits" generated by the gamma trading effort. Both time decay and gamma are negative even if $\sigma_{realized}$ is greater than $\sigma_{implied}$. We shall see later that this does not imply that the trader has lost money.

More generally, the profit or loss (PnL) at time T from any spot trade is given by

$$\text{PnL} = (S_T - S_t) \times N,$$

where S_t is the current value of spot, N is the notional traded, and we maintain the zero interest rates assumption. Therefore the expected profit is

$$\mathbb{E}_t[\text{PnL}] = \mathbb{E}_t[S_T - S_t] \times N$$
$$= 0, \qquad (4.5)$$

where in the second line of (4.5) I have used Equation (2.9). This means that while time decay is always negative, the expected profits to gamma trading are zero. After all, gamma trading is simply a set of spot trades. Thinking of gamma and time decay as two offsetting quantities as described in Section 4.2 can falsely lead one to the conclusion that the expected profits from time decay plus gamma are negative and an option buyer is destined to lose money!

A useful way to correctly understand the profits from gamma hedging an option is using the value function. Suppose that the trader purchases the option and pays a price $V(S_t, t, \sigma_i)$. She then gamma trades by executing a series of delta hedges corresponding to spot and time, as described earlier. A time period δ later, she assesses the change in the value of her portfolio as follows,

$$\text{PnL} = V(S_{t+\delta}, t + \delta) + \sum_{i=1}^{N} (\Delta_i^* - \Delta_{i-1}^*) \times (S_{t+\delta} - S_i) - V(S_t, t) \qquad (4.6)$$

$$= \underbrace{\sum_{i=1}^{N} (\Delta_i^* - \Delta_{i-1}^*)(S_{t+\delta} - S_i)}_{\text{1. Gamma Trading.}} + \underbrace{\Theta(S_t, t, \delta)}_{\text{2. Time Decay.}} + \underbrace{V(S_{t+\delta}, t + \delta) - V(S_t, t + \delta)}_{\text{3. Option Revaluation.}},$$

where in term 2 I use $\Theta(S_t, t, \delta) = V(S_t, t + \delta) - V(S_t, t)$ from Equation (3.1). $\Delta_0^* = 0$. Let us examine each of the terms above in turn.

Term 1 relates to the PnL generated through gamma trading. In the example above there were $N = 3$ spot trades. Initially, the trader sold $\Delta_1^* = 50$ million EUR. Next she sold $\Delta_2^* - \Delta_1^* = 25$ million EUR. Finally she bought $\Delta_3^* - \Delta_2^* = 25$ million EUR. Spot ended at $S_{t+\delta} = 1.37$ and term 1 summed to 500 thousand USD.

I use the notation Δ^* rather than Δ. The reason is that the equation above refers to the delta amount that the trader actually traded, whereas Δ refers to the delta of the option derived using the methods discussed in Chapter 2. Of course, if the trader follows her model exactly, then $\Delta^* = -\Delta$.

The reason that term 1 involves the difference, $\Delta_i - \Delta_{i-1}$, is because the delta hedge that the trader executes at each time step is the change in delta of the option, so that the total notional of EUR she has sold corresponds to the delta of the option.

Term 2 is the time decay term. In the earlier example above, this term was -439 thousand USD.

I refer to term 3 as *option revaluation*. There is no market convention for the name of this term. In our example, spot started and ended at the same point, $S_{t+\delta} = S_t = 1.37$ and therefore the option revaluation term was 0. In general, this is not true. In the scenario where both gamma and time decay are negative, when spot rises, and then rises again, the option revaluation is positive and offsets the negative impact from gamma trading and time decay. In Section 4.5.1, I work through a concrete example that illustrates this point using a 1-week expiry option.

4.5 PnL EXPLAIN

Option traders refer to Equation (4.6) as their *PnL Explain* because it breaks down their trading PnL into its components. It is more accurate to say that this is a subset of a trader's PnL Explain. In reality, there are many more moving parts other than the spot rate and time that we have not yet examined, such as movements in $\sigma_{implied}$ and in *surface*, but that form the remainder of a complete PnL Explain. I return to these topics in later chapters. For now it is sufficient for the reader to understand that if $\sigma_{implied}$ and all other parameters are constant, as they are in the BSM model, then Equation (4.6) is equivalent to a trader's PnL Explain.

4.5.1 Example: Gamma, Time Decay, and PnL Explain for a 1-Week Option

Consider a scenario in which $S_t = 1.37$ on Monday at 3 p.m. London time (10 a.m. New York time). The option trader purchases a 1.37 strike EUR call option with notional 100 million EUR, $\delta = 1$ week expiry and $\sigma_{implied} = 10\%$. Spot then happens to follow the path shown in Figure 4.1. The trader

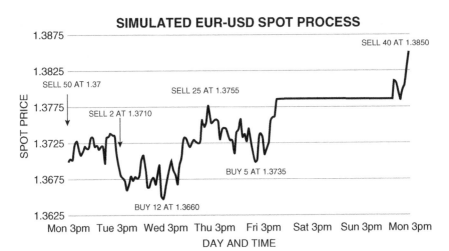

FIGURE 4.1 The figure shows a simulated spot path for EUR-USD over the period of 1 week and the delta hedges associated with the purchase of 100 million EUR of a 1.37 strike call option at 3 p.m. on Monday. I assume that the trader delta hedges just once per day. Initially, the trader sells 50 million EUR. Then, when the probability of an ITM expiry rises, for example, if spot rises or if the option is ITM as time progresses, the trader sells EUR. Similarly, the trader buys EUR when spot falls. She is trading *long gamma*. The chart is overlayed with the spot trades that she executes.

diligently delta hedges her option by executing the spot trades shown in the figure. Her gamma trading PnL, term 1 in Equation (4.6), is given by

$$
\begin{aligned}
\sum_{i=1}^{6} (S_{t+\delta} - S_i)(\Delta_i^* - \Delta_{i-1}^*) = \ & (1.3850 - 1.37) \times -50 \text{ mil EUR} \\
& + (1.3850 - 1.3710) \times -2 \text{ mil EUR} \\
& + (1.3850 - 1.3660) \times 12 \text{ mil EUR} \\
& + (1.3850 - 1.3755) \times -25 \text{ mil EUR} \\
& + (1.3850 - 1.3735) \times 5 \text{ mil EUR} \\
& + (1.3850 - 1.3850) \times -40 \text{ mil EUR} \\
= \ & -730 \text{ thousand EUR.} \quad (4.7)
\end{aligned}
$$

Here, I have not explained where the Δ_i^* values are derived from. For this example I used the BSM formula for Δ from Chapter 10. The reader may skip ahead, use the formula, plugging in $\sigma_{implied} = 10\%$, and confirm the values above. Alternatively, the values above can be calculated approximately but to a high degree of accuracy using a normal distribution, as described in the next feature box.

CALCULATING DELTA USING A NORMAL DISTRIBUTION

On Thursday at 3 p.m. the trader sells 25 million EUR (see Figure 4.1). As an example, I derive this quantity using a normal distribution. The reader may use the following method to confirm the remaining delta trades.

Recall from Equation (3.9) that the standard deviation scales with the square root of time and that $\sigma_{implied} = 10\%$ is an annualized quantity. Therefore, with four days until expiry, the standard deviation is

$$\sigma = \sqrt{\frac{4}{365}} \times 10\% \times 1.3755 = 0.0144,$$

where 1.3755 is the spot level. Applying delta as the probability of an ITM expiry (from Section 2.8) using normal distribution we have

$$\Delta_t \approx \text{Prob}_t(S_T > K) = 1 - N(1.3755, 0.0144)$$

$$= 65\%.$$

Here, $N(\mu, \sigma)$ refers to a normal CDF. I applied Equation (2.9) to find $\mu = 1.3755$.

The delta of the option is 65 million EUR. Note that by Wednesday at 3 p.m. the trader had sold a cumulative total of 40 million EUR. Therefore, she needed to sell 25 million EUR at spot 1.3755 on Thursday.

The time decay PnL, term 2 in Equation (4.6), is simply the value of the option because this example is calculated over the entire lifetime of the option. It is calculated using Equation (3.4),

$$\Theta(S_t, t, \delta) = -\frac{2.1}{100} \times 10\% * \sqrt{7} \times 100 \text{ million EUR} = -761 \text{ thousand USD}.$$

Finally, the option revaluation term, term 3 in Equation (4.6), is given by

$$V(S_{t+\delta}, t + \delta) - V(S_t, t + \delta) = (1.3850 - 1.37) \times 100 \text{ million EUR}$$
$$= 1.5 \text{ million USD.}$$

It is the difference between the intrinsic value of the option with spot at expiry $S_{t+\delta}$ and spot at inception S_t.

The PnL explain is therefore given by

$$\text{PnL} = \underbrace{-730\text{k USD}}_{\text{1. Gamma Trading.}} \underbrace{-761\text{k USD}}_{\text{2. Time Decay.}} \underbrace{+1500\text{k USD}}_{\text{3. Option Revaluation.}}$$

$$= 9 \text{ thousand USD.} \tag{4.8}$$

There are three important points for the reader to note. First, the gamma trading term is negative and so is the time decay term. These terms are offset by the option revaluation term. This example makes clear that when one thinks of the gamma–time decay trade-off, it does not mean that terms 1 and 2 must offset each other in the PnL Explain. The trader makes money when terms 1 and 3 *combined* offset term 2.

Second, note that in this particular example, the trader would have performed much better had she not executed any delta hedges at all! Indeed, had she purchased the option and then not monitored it at all, her PnL would be 739 thousand USD. How can this be possible if every spot trade that she executed has zero expected profit/loss (see Equation 4.5)? This is the topic of the next section.

4.6 DELTA HEDGING AND PnL VARIANCE

The answer to the previous question is simply that it was the luck of the draw. By delta hedging, the trader limited her PnL to 9 thousand USD, but by limiting her upside so she also limited the amount of money that she could lose.

Suppose, for example, that she never delta hedged. Then term 1 is zero. Term 2 is −761 thousand USD regardless of her hedging strategy. Term 3 depends on what spot actually does. In Figure 4.1 it is 1.5 million USD because spot happened to go up to 1.3850, leaving her with 739 thousand USD. Had it gone down instead, and ended anywhere below 1.37, then term 3 would be zero and the trader would have lost 761 thousand USD.

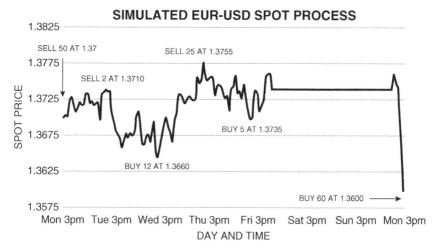

FIGURE 4.2 The figure is identical to Figure 4.1, apart from between Friday and Monday spot is simulated lower to 1.3600 rather than higher.

However, by selling spot, the trader limits her losses even if the option expires OTM. For example, if from Friday to Monday spot went from 1.3735 to 1.3600 (instead of up to 1.3850), as shown in Figure 4.2, then her PnL would have also been 9 thousand USD. See the following calculation.

$$\sum_{i=1}^{6} \times (S_{t+\delta} - S_i)(\Delta_i^* - \Delta_{i-1}^*) = (1.3600 - 1.37) \times -50 \text{ mil EUR}$$
$$+ (1.3600 - 1.3710) \times -2 \text{ mil EUR}$$
$$+ (1.3600 - 1.3660) \times 12 \text{ mil EUR}$$
$$+ (1.3600 - 1.3755) \times -25 \text{ mil EUR}$$
$$+ (1.3600 - 1.3735) \times 5 \text{ mil EUR}$$
$$+ (1.3600 - 1.3650) \times 60 \text{ mil EUR}$$
$$= 770 \text{ thousand EUR}. \qquad (4.9)$$

Her PnL explain is therefore

$$\text{PnL} = \underbrace{770\text{k USD}}_{\text{1. Gamma Trading.}} \underbrace{-761\text{k USD}}_{\text{2. Time Decay.}} \underbrace{+0\text{k USD}}_{\text{3. Portfolio Revaluation.}}$$

$$= 9 \text{ thousand USD}. \qquad (4.10)$$

The important point to note here is that by delta hedging, the trader's PnL is 9 thousand USD regardless of whether the call option expired ITM with spot following the path from Figure 4.1, or OTM with spot following the path from Figure 4.2. Had she not delta hedged, her PnL would have been +739 thousand USD if the option expired ITM at 1.3850[1] or −761k USD had the option expired OTM.

The reader is correct to suspect that I chose the ending spot level of 1.3600 in Figure 4.2 so that the delta hedged case PnL would be 9 thousand USD, equal to that in the case where spot went higher to 1.3850. There are clearly many simulations in which the PnL would be significantly different to 9 thousand USD. However, I chose this example to illustrate that an important feature of delta hedging is to decrease PnL variance. We will see in the BSM model in Chapters 9 and 10 that delta hedging in continuous time is able to diminish the variance of the PnL to zero. In practice, delta hedging dramatically decreases PnL variance, but because implied volatility is itself random and since continuous hedging is not practical, delta hedging cannot decrease this variance all the way to zero.

We saw in Chapter 1 in the context of an ATMS option that delta hedging leaves the trader exposed to volatility only. This is consistent with the arguments in this subsection. PnL variance relating to an option is derived from at least two sources: spot moving and implied volatility changing. By delta hedging, one is able to remove the former and so the overall PnL variance diminishes.

4.7   TRANSACTION COSTS

Practical delta hedging involves transaction costs. In normal markets and in the sizes shown in the previous figures the typical cost would be of the order of 1 pip. In times of higher volatility or in larger size the cost is higher. The total notional of spot trading in Figure 4.1 is 134 million EUR, costing 13.4 thousand USD to transact. Given that the total PnL in this scenario was

---

[1]Note that the if the trader did not delta hedge during the lifetime of the option, then by exercising her option at expiry she would purchase 100 million EUR at 1.37. She would therefore have to execute one delta hedge of selling 100 million EUR in order to lock in her profit.

9 thousand USD it is clear that transaction costs are important. In this case they would have left the trader with a net loss.

4.8   DAILY PnL EXPLAIN

So far we have looked at the PnL Explain of an option over its lifetime. In practice traders construct PnL Explains at the end of each trading day. To do so the trader must apply $\delta = 1$ day to Equation (4.6). Terms 1 and 2 are straightforward to calculate. The trader sold 50 million EUR at 1.3700; 24 hours later the spot rate is $S_{t+\delta} = 1.3710$, so term 1 is -50 thousand USD. Next, term 2 is given by applying Equation (3.5),

$$\Theta(S_t, t, t + 1 \text{ day}, \sigma_i) = V(S_t, t + 1 \text{ day}, \sigma_i) - V(S_t, t, \sigma_i)$$

$$= \frac{2.1}{100} \times 10\% \times (\sqrt{6} - \sqrt{7}) \times N$$

$$= -56 \text{ thousand USD.} \qquad (4.11)$$

Term 3 is more difficult to calculate. Since spot moves from 1.3700 to 1.3710 between Monday and Tuesday, the option goes from being ATMS to ITM. So far, I have only provided formulae to value ATMS options, and not ITM or OTM options. Therefore we are not yet able to calculate term 3. For interested readers, I provide an approximate solution in the next feature box using a normal distribution.

PRICE OF AN OPTION UNDER A NORMAL PDF

On Tuesday at 3 p.m. the trader wishes to value her option, which expires in 6 days. Here, I provide a solution using a normal distribution.

Recall from Equation (3.9) that the standard deviation scales with the square root of time and that $\sigma_{implied} = 10\%$ is an annualized quantity. Therefore, with 6 days until expiry the standard deviation is

$$\sigma = \sqrt{\frac{6}{365}} \times 10\% \times 1.3710 = 0.0176,$$

(Continued)

where 1.3710 is the spot level. Applying Equation (2.2),

$$V(S_t, K, t) = \int_{-\infty}^{\infty} \max(x - K, 0) f_t(x) dx$$

$$= \frac{1}{\sqrt{2\pi\sigma^2}} \int_K^{\infty} (x - K) \exp\left(-\frac{(x - S_t)^2}{2\sigma^2}\right) dx$$

$$= (S_t - K)\,\mathrm{Prob}_t(S_T > K) + \frac{\sigma}{\sqrt{2\pi}} \exp\left(-\frac{(K - S_t)^2}{2\sigma^2}\right)$$

$$= (S_t - K)\Delta_t + \frac{\sigma}{\sqrt{2\pi}} \exp\left(-\frac{(K - S_t)^2}{2\sigma^2}\right).$$

The option revaluation term is then calculated using this equation,

$$V(S_{t+\delta}, t+\delta) - V(S_t, t+\delta) = (S_{t+\delta} - K)\Delta_{t+\delta} + \frac{\sigma}{\sqrt{2\pi}} \exp\left(-\frac{(K - S_{t+\delta})^2}{2\sigma^2}\right)$$

$$-(S_t - K)\Delta_t + \frac{\sigma}{\sqrt{2\pi}} \exp\left(-\frac{(K - S_t)^2}{2\sigma^2}\right)$$

$$= 754k\ USD - 701k\ USD = 54k\ USD.$$

The one-day PnL Explain is then

$$\mathrm{PnL} = \underbrace{-50k\ USD}_{} \quad \underbrace{-56k\ USD}_{} \quad \underbrace{+54k\ USD}_{}$$

1. Gamma Trading. 2. Time Decay. 3. Portfolio Revaluation.

$$= -52\ \text{thousand USD}. \tag{4.12}$$

It is intuitive that the trader has lost money. She is long the option but the realized volatility has been low. The spot rate has only moved by 10 pips, from 1.3700 to 1.3710. Recall from Section 1.5.4 that a daily return of $\ln(1.3710/1.37) = 0.07\%$ corresponds to an annualized realized volatility of just $0.07 \times 16\% = 1.16\%$, far below $\sigma_{implied}$ of 10%. It is intuitive then that she has made back about 10% of her time decay via terms 1 and 3.

4.9   THE GAMMA PROFILE

It is important to understand the variation of $\Gamma(S_t, t, \sigma_i)$ with S_t, t and $\sigma_{implied}$ to risk manage an option over its lifetime. I refer to these variations as *gamma profiles*. Let us begin with S_t.

4.9.1   Gamma and Spot

The reader is familiar with the delta profile of an option shown by the light gray line in Figure 4.3. Recall from Equation (4.2) that $\Gamma(S_t, t, \sigma_i)$ is the partial derivative of $\Delta(S_t, t, \sigma_i)$ with respect to S_t. It is therefore clear that $\Gamma(S_t, t, \sigma_i)$ should look like the dark gray line in Figure 4.3. It is zero where when the light gray line is flat (when the option is deep ITM or deep OTM) and it peaks when the light gray line is steepest (when the option is ATMS in our model of Chapter 2).

The key takeaway here is that $\Gamma(S_t, t, \sigma_i)$ peaks when $\Delta(S_t, t, \sigma_i)$ changes most quickly for a small change in S_t and this happens when the option is ATMS, $S_t \approx K$.

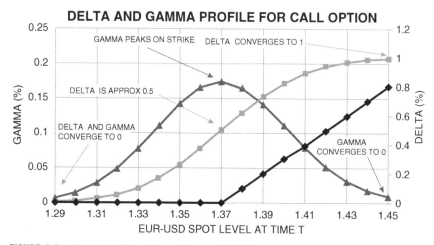

FIGURE 4.3   The black line shows the payoff of the 1.37 strike call option. The light gray line shows $\Delta(S_t, t, \sigma_i)$ (right axis). Recall that $\Delta(S_t, t, \sigma_i)$ is 0 when the option is deep OTM $S_t \ll K$, approximately 50% when the option is ATMS $S_t = K$, and 100% when the option is deep ITM $S_t \gg K$. The dark gray line shows the gamma profile, $\Gamma(S_t, t, \sigma_i)$ (left axis). $\Gamma(S_t, t, \sigma_i)$ is zero when the option is deep OTM, and zero when the option is deep ITM. It peaks when $S_t \approx K$.

4.9.2 Gamma and Implied Volatility

Figure 4.4 is identical to Figure 4.3 except that it corresponds to a lower level of σ_i. There are two important points to note.

First, the light gray line $\Delta(S_t, t, \sigma_i)$ is more steep. The intuition here is straightforward. If $S_t = 1.39$ and σ_i is low, then $\text{Prob}(S_T > K)$ is higher than if σ_i is high because when σ_i is low spot is less likely to move back through strike K. Therefore, the change in $\Delta(S_t, t, \sigma_i)$ in S_t moving from 1.37 to 1.39 is larger when σ_i is low than when it is high. Correspondingly, the light gray line is more steep, and $\Gamma(S_t, t, \sigma_i)$ has a higher peak. One can make an analogous argument to explain the steepness of the light gray line for spot moving from 1.35 to 1.37.

Second, while $\Gamma(S_t, t, \sigma_i)$ has a higher peak, it takes higher values over a smaller range in S_t. $\Gamma(1.29, t, \sigma_i)$ is close to zero, as is $\Gamma(1.31, t, \sigma_i)$. Therefore $\Gamma(S_t, t, \sigma_i)$ over the ranges beyond 1.29 and 1.31 is also close to zero. This is not true if σ_i is high.

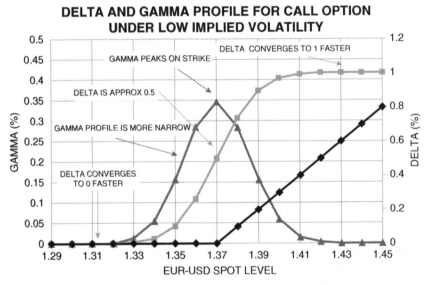

FIGURE 4.4 The light gray line shows $\Delta(S_t, t, \sigma_i)$ and the dark gray line shows $\Gamma(S_t, t, \sigma_i)$ for a lower level of σ_i than Figure 4.3. The main point to note is that $\Delta(S_t, t, \sigma_i)$ has a steeper gradient over a narrower range in S_t. Correspondingly, $\Gamma(S_t, t, \sigma_i)$ has a higher peak and is also more narrow.

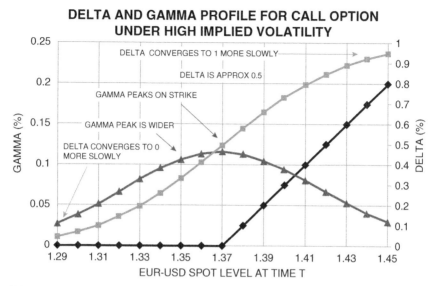

FIGURE 4.5 The light gray line shows $\Delta(S_t, t, \sigma_i)$ and the dark gray line shows $\Gamma(S_t, t, \sigma_i)$ for a higher level of σ_i than Figure 4.3. The main point to note is that $\Delta(S_t, t, \sigma_i)$ has a flatter gradient over a wider range in S_t. Correspondingly, $\Gamma(S_t, t, \sigma_i)$ has a lower peak and is also wider.

Finally, Figure 4.5 shows $\Delta(S_t, t, \sigma_i)$ and $\Gamma(S_t, t, \sigma_i)$ corresponding to a higher level of σ_i. $\Delta(S_t, t, \sigma_i)$, shown in light gray, is less steeply upward sloping, and $\Gamma(S_t, t, \sigma_i)$, shown in dark gray, is flatter and wider than in Figure 4.4.

4.9.3 Gamma and Time

Recall from Equation (3.10) that, subject to some assumptions, the implied standard deviation of the spot PDF is given by $\sigma_i \sqrt{n/365}$, where n is the number of calendar days until expiry. Equation (3.9) provided the reason that this standard deviation grows proportionally to the square root of time, or expiry days. This relationship tells us that σ_i and time are interchangeable when it comes to calculating the spot PDF. That is, for example, doubling σ_i is the same as quadrupling the number of calendar days until expiry.

The relationship between $\Gamma(S_t, t, \sigma_i)$ and t is therefore very similar to the relationship between $\Gamma(S_t, t, \sigma_i)$ and σ_i. As time progresses and the time until expiry of an option diminishes, its $\Delta(S_t, t, \sigma_i)$ and $\Gamma(S_t, t, \sigma_i)$ profiles go from those drawn in Figure 4.5 through to Figure 4.4.

The key point to note here is that the $\Gamma(S_t, t, \sigma_i)$ profile of a shorter dated option with $\sigma_i = x$ and n_{short} expiry days looks like that of a longer dated option with $\sigma_i = x\sqrt{n_{short}/n_{long}}$ and n_{long} expiry days. Equivalently, one can generate identical $\Gamma(S_t, t, \sigma_i)$ profiles by lowering σ_i or decreasing the time to expiry.

The argument presented in this subsection explains why option traders often refer to short-dated contracts, typically those with approximately one month or less as *gamma contracts*. A short-dated contract is equivalent to one with low σ_i and Figure 4.4 shows that such contracts have higher peaks in their $\Gamma(S_t, t, \sigma_i)$ profiles.

4.9.4 Total Gamma

A common misconception based on the earlier analysis is that shorter dated options or equivalently options with lower σ_i have *more gamma* in some sense. While it is true that the peak in $\Gamma(S_t, t, \sigma_i)$, at $S_t \approx K$, is larger the nearer the expiry date of the option or the lower σ_i, it is also true that $\Gamma(S_t, t, \sigma_i)$ for such an option is smaller when $S_t \neq K$.

If we define the *total gamma* as its integral, or average, over all spot space, it is straightforward to show that this is the same for every option, regardless of its expiry date or σ_i,

$$\int_0^\infty \Gamma(S, t, \sigma_i)dS = \int_0^\infty \frac{\partial \Delta(S, t, \sigma_i)}{\partial S}dS$$
$$= \Delta(\infty, t, \sigma_i) - \Delta(0, t, \sigma_i)$$
$$= 1,$$

assuming that S_t is never negative. In words, the delta of every option goes from 0 when it is deep OTM to 1 when it is deep ITM, and gamma is the change in delta. A better statement is that shorter dated ATMS options have more localized gamma than longer dated ATMS options.

4.10 TRADER'S SUMMARY

- Gamma $\Gamma(S_t, t, \sigma_i)$ is the change in delta $\Delta(S_t, t, \sigma_i)$ for a change in the spot rate S_t. Mathematically it is defined as the partial derivative of $\Delta(S_t, t, \sigma_i)$ with respect to S_t.

- Option traders typically scale gamma so that it reflects the change in the delta in units of the base currency for a 1% log return. The scaled quantity is called trader's gamma, $\Gamma_{trader}(S_t, t, \sigma_i)$.
- Traders frequently speak of gamma–time decay trade-offs. In fact, a PnL Explain shows that time decay offsets gamma trading plus option revaluation.
- Traders typically calculate PnL Explains on a daily basis.
- Delta hedging involves multiple zero expected return transactions.
- The two main sources of PnL variance associated with an option are spot moving and σ_i changing. Delta hedging removes the PnL variance associated with spot moving.
- Delta hedging involves often significant transaction costs.
- The $\Gamma(S_t, t, \sigma_i)$ profile depends on σ_i. If σ_i is high, then $\Gamma(S_t, t, \sigma_i)$ viewed as a function of S_t is flatter and wider. If σ_i is low, then $\Gamma(S_t, t, \sigma_i)$ is narrower and more peaked.
- The $\Gamma(S_t, t, \sigma_i)$ profile depends on the time/number of days to expiry n. Since the standard deviation of the PDF is given by $\sigma_i\sqrt{n/365}$, time passing, or n decreasing, is equivalent to decreasing σ_i.
- The peak gamma is higher for a shorter dated option than for a longer dated option. However, while it is correct to say that shorter dated options have more gamma when they are ATMS, it is not correct to say that they have more gamma. The total gamma of every option is the same because the delta goes from 0 to 1 across all spot space.

CHAPTER 5

The Basic Greeks: Vega

Vega describes how an option price changes with implied volatility. Loosely put, a vega position of long 100 thousand USD in EUR-USD, for example, means that if implied volatility rises by 1%, the option trader's PnL is +100 thousand USD.

When discussing vega, the trader must make clear which implied volatility she is calculating the sensitivity with respect to. Most commonly, traders take the derivative with respect to $\sigma_{implied}$ and instead refer to Black-Scholes vega. However, even this remains unclear. In later chapters, we will see that in practice $\sigma_{implied}$ is itself a function of K, $\sigma_{implied}(K)$. Therefore, one must ask if the derivative is with respect to $\sigma_{implied}(K)$ where K corresponds to the option in question, or whether K corresponds to a standard contract, such as the ATM, or if it corresponds to something else. To avoid ambiguity, in this chapter I take derivatives with respect to σ_i, which the reader may continue to interpret as the standard deviation of the PDF.

Next, it is interesting to note that in every model, spot moves, which gives delta and gamma their importance, and time moves forward, which gives theta its importance. However, the nature of movements in σ_i is less clear. For example, the concept of $\sigma_{implied}$ originates from the BSM model, and yet this model assumed that $\sigma_{implied}$ does not change, thereby making Black-Scholes vega a redundant concept within the BSM framework. In so-called *local volatility* models, σ_i moves but only in a manner deterministically linked to S_t. All hedging can be done with spot, and so again vega is a redundant concept (Gatheral, 2006, provides a detailed practitioner's guide). Finally, so-called *stochastic volatility* models allow σ_i to move in a random manner and so vega becomes an important Greek once again.

In practice, stochastic volatility models are most relevant because σ_i changes many times each day and in a manner that is only correlated with and not determined by spot. This makes it important for option traders to monitor their vega positions. The movements in σ_i also give rise to *smile* or *surface* (see Chapters 7 and 8).

The remainder of this chapter discusses the concept of vega and its variations with expiry date and spot.

5.1 VEGA

Vega, v_t, is the sensitivity of the price of the option with respect to σ_i,

$$v_t = v(S_t, t, \sigma_i) = \frac{\partial V(S_t, t, \sigma_i)}{\partial \sigma_i}. \tag{5.1}$$

We can gain an understanding of how this function looks. Recall Equation (3.11) told us the approximate value of an ATMS option in the context of the normal model as a function of σ_i^*, where σ_i^* represented the annualized standard deviation of a normal distribution. Differentiating this equation with respect to σ_i^* gives us

$$v(S_t = K, t, \sigma_i) = \frac{2.1}{100} \sqrt{n} \times N \tag{5.2}$$

for an ATMS option.

Similarly, note that differentiating Equation (3.4) with respect to $\sigma_{implied}$ yields the exact same result but for an ATM option. That is, the Black-Scholes vega, v_{BS}, for an ATM option with zero interest rates,

$$v_{BS}(S_t, t, \sigma_{implied}) = \frac{2.1}{100} \sqrt{n} \times N, \tag{5.3}$$

where $S_t = K e^{\frac{1}{2}\sigma_{implied}^2 \tau}$.

These equations tell us that v_t increases in proportion to the square root of the expiry date in both the normal model and the BSM log-normal model. The important point to take away is that longer dated options have larger v_t than shorter expiry options.

CALCULATING v_{BS}: AN EXAMPLE

Let us apply Equation (5.3) to calculate v_{BS} for a 1-year expiry option on EUR-USD with notional $N = 100$ million EUR. We find that $v_{BS} = 0.021 \times \sqrt{365} \times 100$mio EUR $= 400$k EUR. If the EUR-USD spot rate is at 1.37, then this is equivalent to 548 thousand USD of vega. Increasing $\sigma_{implied}$ by 1%[a] raises the price of this option by 400 thousand EUR, or 548 thousand USD. It is worth reiterating that this equation only applies to ATM options and even this is an approximation. I discuss ITM and OTM options later in the chapter.

Further, note that v_{BS} is independent of σ_i for ATMS options. Therefore, if, for example, $\sigma_i = 10\%$, then the price of the ATMS call option or put option is 4 million EUR.

---

[a]Traders often refer to a one-percentage-point move in $\sigma_{implied}$ as a move of 1 *vol*.

Next, I discuss two methods through which one can intuitively understand v_t. The first is through the PDF of the spot distribution (introduced in Chapter 1) and the second is through gamma trading (introduced in Section 4.1).

5.2   UNDERSTANDING VEGA VIA THE PDF

Figure 5.1 will look familiar from Chapter 1. The key point to reemphasize here is that the larger σ_i, the wider the PDF of the spot distribution that is priced into options, and the higher the expected payoff of the straddle. Therefore, as σ_i increases, so does the price of the option, and therefore $v_t > 0$.

5.3   UNDERSTANDING VEGA VIA GAMMA TRADING

Next, reconsider the gamma trading argument of Section 4.1. σ_i reflects option traders' (risk adjusted) expectations of $\sigma_{realized}$ over the lifetime of the

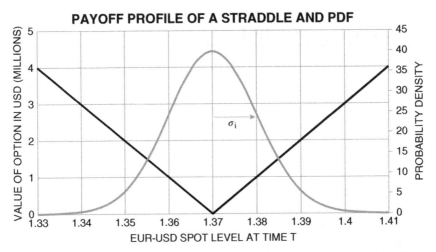

FIGURE 5.1 The figure shows the payoff of a straddle option strategy and the PDF of EUR-USD overlayed. The larger σ_i, the higher the probability that EUR-USD moves away from 1.37 and the owner of the straddle receives a larger payoff. The option price is therefore increasing in σ_i.

trade. The higher that $\sigma_{realized}$ is over the lifetime of the option, the greater the opportunity for the trader to gamma trade—buy spot when it falls, and sell spot when it rises—and the greater the value of owning the option. Therefore, if expectations of $\sigma_{realized}$ rise, σ_i rises, and so does the price that the trader is willing to pay to purchase options, because she is able to earn more in gamma trading and portfolio revaluation. The result is that v_t is positive. The owner of an option is said to be *long vega*.

5.4 VEGA OF AN ATMS OPTION ACROSS TENORS

Equation (5.2) tells us that v_t for an ATMS option rises with the square root of the number of days to expiry n in the normal model and Equation (5.3) told us that a similar result holds true for ATM options in the BSM log-normal model. One way to understand why this is true is to consider how the PDF of spot changes with n.

The standard deviation of the implied PDF for an option with n days until expiry is given by $\sigma_i \sqrt{n/365}$ as exhibited by Equation (3.10). Hence, as discussed in Section 1.5.1, in the case of $n = 365$, or 1 year, σ_i is, up to some

caveats relating to risk neutrality and smile, the standard deviation of the 1-year PDF. I continue to ignore the dependence of σ_i on n until Chapter 6.

It is clear that when n is large, a given change in σ_i has a larger effect on the standard deviation of the implied PDF than when n is small. Therefore, longer dated expiry options are more sensitive to σ_i than shorter expiries; they have larger values of v_t. The increase is proportional to the square root of n. The argument here is very similar to that made in the context of theta in Section 3.1.3. The argument can be understood in the context of a normal distribution via Equation (3.11).

Although it may appear reasonable to conclude at this stage that longer dated contracts are more *risky* than shorter dated contracts because they carry higher v_t, this is not necessarily true. When we study the dependence of σ_i itself on n in Chapter 6 we will see that changes in σ_i are typically larger for small n than for large n. These changes can offset the fact that v_t increases with n.

5.5 VEGA AND SPOT

Figure 5.2 shows the vega profile of a call option by which I refer to $v(S_t, t, \sigma_i)$ plotted as a function of S_t.

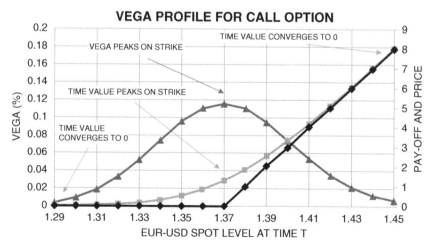

FIGURE 5.2 The figure shows the vega profile (dark gray, left axis), price (light gray, right axis) and payoff (black, right axis) of a call option. The vega peaks at $S_t \approx K$. Here, I use a 1-month expiry, $\sigma_i = 8\%$, and the BSM function.

Like the theta and gamma profiles, the vega profile peaks when the option is approximately ATMS, $S_t \approx K$. Deep ITM and deep OTM options have little vega. There are several ways to understand this.

Start at the limit where $\sigma_i = 0$. The price of the option is then simply its intrinsic value, the black line in Figure 5.2. If we raise σ_i to x%, the price of the option rises. For example, the light gray line in Figure 5.2 corresponds to x = 8. The change in price is exactly equal to the time value of the option valued using $\sigma_i = x\%$, or $\Theta_{tv}(S_t, t, \sigma_i)$; Equation (2.19) defined the time value as the light gray line minus the black line in (5.2). Recall from Section 3.1.2 that the peak in time value occurs when $S_t \approx K$ and then diminishes. By definition,

$$V(S_t, t, \sigma_i)|_{\sigma_i = x\%} = V(S_t, T) + \int_0^{x\%} \frac{\partial V(S_t, t, \sigma_i)}{\partial \sigma_i} d\sigma_i,$$

and therefore

$$\Theta_{tv}(S_t, t, \sigma_i) = \int_0^{x\%} v(S_t, t, \sigma_i) d\sigma_i,$$

Since $\Theta_{tv}(S_t, t, \sigma_i)$ peaks at $S_t \approx K$, we know that $\int_0^{x\%} v(S_t, t, \sigma_i) d\sigma_i$ peaks at $S_t \approx K$, for any x.

The reader may wish to prove that $v(S_t, t, \sigma_i)$ itself and not just its integral peaks at $S_t \approx K$ and that this is true for all values of σ_i. I provide a formal proof of this in the feature box. Next, I explain the intuition that underlies this proof.

Figure 5.3 shows the value function $V(S_t, t, \sigma_i)$ at two different levels of σ_i, namely σ_1 and σ_2, where $\sigma_1 < \sigma_2$. In the figure, I choose $\sigma_1 = 8\%$, $\sigma_2 = 12\%$ and a 1-month expiry. The light gray line shows $V(S_t, t, \sigma_1)$ and the dark gray line shows $V(S_t, t, \sigma_2)$. It is intuitive that the point of maximum $v(S_t, t, \sigma_1)$ occurs at the value of S_t where $V(S_t, t, \sigma_2) - V(S_t, t, \sigma_1)$ is largest because by the Taylor theorem,

$$V(S_t, t, \sigma_2) - V(S_t, t, \sigma_1) = v(S_t, t, \sigma_1)(\sigma_2 - \sigma_1) + \text{higher order terms}.$$

The *higher order terms* are smallest when $\sigma_2 - \sigma_1$ is small, but here I use 12% and 8% respectively so that the gap between the value functions in the figure can be clearly seen.

Start at S_0. If $\Delta(S_0, t, \sigma_2)$ is greater than $\Delta(S_0, t, \sigma_1)$, then we know that if we move to point S_1 just to the right of S_0, the difference between the value functions is greater than at S_0. That is, $V(S_1, t, \sigma_2) - V(S_1, t, \sigma_1) > V(S_0, t, \sigma_2) - V(S_0, t, \sigma_1)$ and therefore S_0 cannot be the peak value of

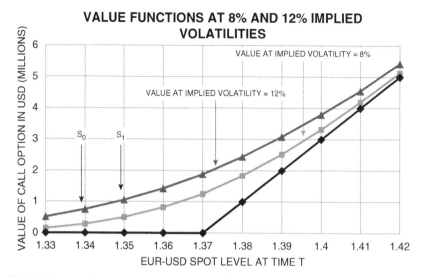

FIGURE 5.3 The figure shows the payoff profile of a $K = 1.37$ call option (black) and its value function assuming 1-month expiry and $\sigma_2 = 12\%$ (dark gray) and $\sigma_1 = 8\%$ (light gray). In moving from $S_0 = 1.34$ to $S_1 = 1.35$ we see that the gap between the light gray line and dark gray line widens. The reason is that the steepness of the dark gray line, $\Delta(S_0, t, 12\%)$, is greater than that of the light gray line, $\Delta(S_0, t, 8\%)$. Therefore, $v(S_1, t, 8\%) > v(S_0, t, 8\%)$ and S_0 is not the vega peak. Continuing the logic tells us that the vega peak must occur when $\Delta(S_t, t, 12\%) = \Delta(S_t, t, 8\%)$. We know from previous chapters that this is true at $S_t \approx 1.37$ where $\Delta(S_t, t, 12\%) \approx \Delta(S_t, t, 8\%) \approx 0.5$.

$v(S_t, t, \sigma_1)$. Therefore, we must keep moving to the right until $\Delta(S_t, t, \sigma_1) = \Delta(S_t, t, \sigma_2)$. However, we know from previous chapters that this occurs at $S_t \approx K$ where $\Delta \approx 0.5$ regardless of σ_i. Hence the peak in $v(S_t, t, \sigma_1)$ occurs at $S_t \approx K$.

VEGA PEAKS WHEN AN OPTION IS ATMS, $S_t = K$. PROOF IS VIA DELTA

Start with

$$\int_{\sigma_1}^{\sigma_2} v(S, t, \sigma_i)\,d\sigma_i = V(S, t, \sigma_2) - V(S, t, \sigma_1)$$

(Continued)

This is true for any values of σ_2 and σ_1 and $\sigma_2 > \sigma_1$. We wish to find the value of S at which the left-hand side of the above equation is maximum. Differentiating with respect to S, we have

$$\frac{\partial}{\partial S} \int_{\sigma_1}^{\sigma_2} v(S,t,\sigma_i) d\sigma_i = \frac{\partial}{\partial S}(V(S,t,\sigma_2) - V(S,t,\sigma_1)).$$

$$= \Delta(S,t,\sigma_2) - \Delta(S,t,\sigma_1)$$

$$= 0 \text{ if } S = K. \tag{5.4}$$

In the last line I use the approximation and result from Chapter 2 that $\Delta(S_t,t,\sigma_i) = 0.5$ for an ATMS option regardless of the level of σ_i. Next, differentiate with respect to S once more:

$$\frac{\partial^2}{\partial S^2} \int_{\sigma_1}^{\sigma_2} v(S,t,\sigma_i) d\sigma_i = \frac{\partial}{\partial S}(\Delta(S,t,\sigma_2) - \Delta(S,t,\sigma_1))$$

$$= \Gamma(S,t,\sigma_2) - \Gamma(S,t,\sigma_1)$$

$$< 0 \text{ if } S_t = K. \tag{5.5}$$

In the last line I use the result from Subsection 4.9.2 that at $S = K$, $\Gamma(S,t,\sigma_i)$ is lower if σ_i is higher.

Since Equations (5.4) and (5.5) hold for any $\sigma_2 > \sigma_1$, we have found that $v(S,t,\sigma_i)$ is maximum at $S_t = K$. More generally, this holds at $S_t \approx K$.

Second, reconsider Jensen's Inequality from Chapter 2. When an option is deep ITM or deep OTM, the probability distribution largely covers the area of the pay-off that is linear. The price is therefore insensitive to σ_i and $v(S_t,t,\sigma_i)$ is small for $S_t \ll K$ or $S_t \gg K$. The opposite is true around the point of maximum concavity in the payoff function $S_t \approx K$.

5.6 DEPENDENCE OF VEGA ON IMPLIED VOLATILITY

Figure 5.4 shows the vega profile for a 1 month expiry option with $\sigma_i = 4\%$. There are two important features to note.

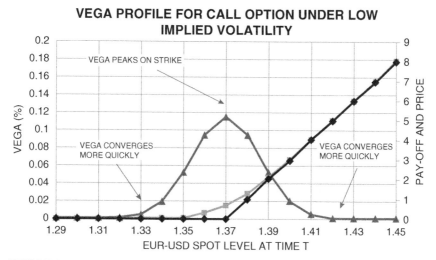

FIGURE 5.4 The figure shows the vega profile (dark gray), price (light gray), and payoff (black) of a call option. The vega peaks around $S_t \approx K$. Here, I use a 1-month expiry and $\sigma_i = 4\%$. The vega profile is narrower than that in Figure 5.2 and the peak is also lower.

First, the height of the vega peak is around 0.15%, identical to the vega peak in Figure 5.2 where $\sigma_i = 8\%$. That is, when $S_t \approx K$, v does not depend on σ_i. This result follows directly from Equations (5.2) and (5.3) where the reader should note that there is no dependence on σ_i or $\sigma_{implied}$. Second, the vega profile is narrower than that in Figure 5.2.

5.7 VEGA PROFILES APPLIED IN PRACTICAL OPTIONS TRADING

It is important for options traders to understand vega profiles in order to plan for how their option portfolios will evolve. Consider the following example.

First, consider a portfolio consisting of a long 1-month expiry EUR call option with $K = 1.37$, $\sigma_i = 8\%$ and notional of 100 million EUR. Suppose $S_t = 1.35$ and the trader is waiting for US non-farm payroll numbers, and she has purchased the EUR call expecting the data to be weak (hence she expects EUR-USD will rise). She turns out to be correct and EUR-USD indeed rises from 1.35 to 1.37. Figure 5.2 tells us that she gets longer vega because the option goes from OTM to ATMS. She is now more exposed to movements in σ_i than she had been. In fact, her v exposure has gone from about 9k EUR to close to 12k EUR.

Typically, after an economic data release such as US non-farm payrolls, σ_i goes down. The reason is that the market anticipates the additional realized volatility from the release (more on this later) and then lowers σ_i once that data has been incorporated into the spot price. This behavior could cost the trader. Not only is she long vega, but she has *derived* even longer vega on the spot move, and σ_i is falling. It is important that the trader anticipate this possibility before purchasing the option.

So-called vega derives can cause significant gains and losses for option traders. Traders often manage these derives using additonal Greeks, known as *vanna* and *volgamma*. This is the topic of the next chapter.

5.8   VEGA AND PnL EXPLAIN

Recall Equation (4.6) provided a breakdown or explanation of the PnL of an option position associated with time progressing. The main components were gamma trading, time decay, and option revaluation. Given the knowledge we have gained in this chapter, namely that options are sensitive to movements in σ_i and that σ_i typically changes many times in a day, we must add terms related to vega to our PnL explain.

Let σ_i take initial value $\sigma_{i,t}$. At a later time $t + \delta$ its value is denoted by $\sigma_{i,t+\delta}$. Appending Equation (4.6) we have

$$\text{PnL} = V(S_{t+\delta}, t + \delta, \sigma_{i,t+\delta}) + \sum_{i=1}^{N}(\Delta_i^* - \Delta_{i-1}^*) \times (S_{t+\delta} - S_i) - V(S_t, t, \sigma_{i,t})$$

$$= \underbrace{\sum_{i=1}^{N}(\Delta_i^* - \Delta_{i-1}^*)(S_{t+\delta} - S_i)}_{\text{1. Gamma Trading.}} + \underbrace{\Theta(S_t, t, \delta)}_{\text{2. Time Decay.}} \qquad (5.6)$$

$$+ \underbrace{V(S_{t+\delta}, t + \delta, \sigma_{i,t}) - V(S_t, t + \delta, \sigma_{i,t})}_{\text{3. Option Revaluation.}}$$

$$+ \underbrace{V(S_{t+\delta}, t + \delta, \sigma_{i,t+\delta}) - V(S_{t+\delta}, t + \delta, \sigma_i)}_{\text{4. Vega Revaluation.}}.$$

There is an important subtlety that the reader should note here. If instead of σ_i, we use the BSM function for V_t and $\sigma_{implied}$ corresponding to the specific strike option in consideration, then the previous equation forms a complete PnL explanation and there are no further terms. I continue to assume zero interest rates. I describe this in more detail in later chapters. However, any other definition of implied volatility leads to additional terms. For example, in most practical application, traders use the BSM function $V = V_{BS}$ and $\sigma_{implied}$ corresponding to the ATM option. In that case we must consider the options smile. This is the topic of Chapters 7 and 8.

5.9 TRADER'S SUMMARY

- Vega, $v(S_t, t, \sigma_i)$, represents the sensitivity of the option price to σ_i.
- $v(S_t, t, \sigma_i)$ increases with the the number of expiry days n. The reason is that the standard deviation of the PDF is $\sigma_i \sqrt{n}$ and so a given change in σ_i has a bigger affect when n is large.
- $v(S_t, t, \sigma_i)$ is largest when $S_t \approx K$ and the option is ATMS. It is smaller when options are deep ITM ($S_t \gg K$) or deep OTM ($S_t \ll K$).
- For an ATM option, v_t is independent of σ_i. However, when the option is OTM or ITM, a higher σ_i corresponds to higher v_t.

CHAPTER 6

Implied Volatility and Term Structure

I introduced the concept of *implied volatility*, $\sigma_{implied}$, in Chapter 1. The objective in this chapter is to deepen our understanding of this fundamental quantity's use in practical options trading. There are two main ideas to understand.

The first is the definition of $\sigma_{implied}$. Rebonato (2004) famously and appropriately described $\sigma_{implied}$ as "the one number to put in the wrong formula to get the right price of plain-vanilla options." I explain what he means by this and why, despite this description, $\sigma_{implied}$ remains the most commonly used metric in practical trading.

The second relates to the fact that $\sigma_{implied}$ is typically a function of the expiry date T. For example, an option trader may face the situation where the 1-week contract trades at $\sigma_{implied} = 10\%$, the 1-month contract trades at 9%, the 6-month contract trades at 10%, and the 1-year contract at 11%. This expiry-based variation in implied volatility is known as *term structure*. More appropriate notation is therefore $\sigma_{implied}(T)$ and this is the notation that I use henceforth.

Most modeling of the term structure references ATMF options. I continue to assume zero foreign and domestic interest rates so ATMF and ATMS options are identical. It is reasonable for the reader to continue to assume that the ideas apply to ATMS options at this stage. However, note that when quoting prices, option traders refer to ATM options by default, unless otherwise specified. I describe how to adjust between ATM and ATMF in the next chapter and the reader need not be concerned about the subtle differences to understand the concepts here.

Given the dependence of $\sigma_{implied}(T)$ on T, option traders may ask questions such as, why does the term structure have a particular shape?

What does this shape imply about future volatility? How does the term structure move over time and in different market conditions? Or how do traders build the term structure in practice? This chapter provides a framework to answer these and other related questions. I discuss the *daily forward volatility* approach to setting the term structure and also several approaches to describing its movements, such as flat vega, weighted vega, and beta-weighted vega. Finally, I tie together many of the ideas discussed by turning to the widely used *GARCH* model.

6.1 IMPLIED VOLATILITY, $\sigma_{implied}$

Recall from Section 2.4 and Equation (2.5) that the price of an option, V_t, is given by plugging S_t, t, σ_i, and parameters ϕ into a value function $V(S_t, t, \sigma_i, \phi)$. Black and Scholes (1973) suggested such a function. The BSM formula says that

$$V_t = V(S_t, t, \phi) = V_{BS}(S_t, t, \sigma_{implied}(T)). \tag{6.1}$$

It is not important to know the functional form of $V_{BS}(S_T, t, \sigma_{implied}(T))$ at this stage, although interested readers may skip to Chapter 9 for a preview. The important point is that we have now defined $\sigma_{implied}(T)$; it is the number that one must insert into the Black-Scholes function, V_{BS}, to match the traded price of the option, corresponding to a particular expiry date and strike. This may seem confusing at first, but it can be understood via the following example.

Suppose that the EUR-USD spot rate is 1.37. Two traders agree to trade between themselves a 1-month EUR-USD call option with strike 1.37 and notional of 100 million EUR at a price of 1.5 million USD that the option buyer must pay to the option seller. To calculate the $\sigma_{implied}(T)$ at which they are trading they take the following two steps. First, they put $S_t = 1.37$, $T = 1$ month (and interest rate parameters that we shall discuss later) into the function V_{BS}. Next, they try different values of $\sigma_{implied}(T)$ in the function V_{BS} until they find the (unique) one that gives them 0.015 as the output (since 0.015×100 million $= 1.5$ million). Suppose that this number turns out to be 10%. The traders therefore have a choice. They can say that they can agree to trade at 1.5 million USD in premium, or they can agree to trade at a $\sigma_{implied}(1$ month$)$ of 10%. Since they both understand that market convention is to calculate option prices using the function $V_{BS}(S_t, t, \sigma_{implied}(T))$,

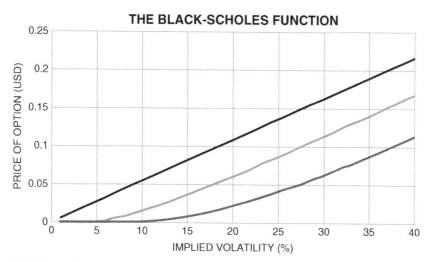

FIGURE 6.1 The figure shows that the price of a 1-year expiry option rises as $\sigma_{implied}$(1 year) rises. I set EUR-USD $S_t = 1.37$. The black line shows $K = 1.37$, the light gray line shows $K = 1.50$ and the dark gray line shows $K = 1.70$. In this chapter we learn that the mapping between $\sigma_{implied}(T)$ and the option price is carried out via the Black-Scholes-Merton function.

they can speak in terms of premiums or $\sigma_{implied}(T)$. Figure 6.1 illustrates V_{BS} by providing a mapping from $\sigma_{implied}$(1 year) to the option price for three different values of K.

In the FX market, participants primarily speak in terms of $\sigma_{implied}(T)$. Chapters 1 and 2 already provided some reasons for this relating to making relative value decisions about the spot PDF. However, another important reason is practical. It is that $\sigma_{implied}(T)$ is less sensitive to moves in the spot rate than the cash premium. The next feature box illustrates this point via an example of a typical FX option trade.

In short, so far we have learned that $\sigma_{implied}(T)$ is simply a number that when put into $V_{BS}(S_t, t, \sigma_{implied}(T))$ provides the correct premium of the option. The functional form of $V_{BS}(S_t, t, \sigma_{implied}(T))$ originates from the Black-Scholes model. If the Black-Scholes model provided the true description of the dynamics of the underlying security, EUR-USD spot for example, then the economic meaning of $\sigma_{implied}(T)$ would be clear. It is the annualized standard deviation of the PDF of the log spot return over horizon T, as discussed in more detail in Section 1.5.1. However, given the empirical evidence that the Black-Scholes model does not capture features of spot returns such as skewness and kurtosis, the ideas presented in Section 1.5.1 can only be treated as an approximation. Nevertheless, these ideas are a very useful approximation and allow traders to make trading and risk management decisions quickly and without resorting to computation.

TRADING AN FX OPTION OVER THE COUNTER (OTC)—PART 1

A customer wishes to trade a 3-month EUR call option with $K = 1.37$ and notional of 100 million EUR. At the time of asking, the EUR-USD spot rate is 1.37. He contacts a market maker, usually a bank, to ask for a price. The options trader at the bank quotes 10%/10.3%. This means that she stands ready to buy at her *bid* of $\sigma_{implied}$(3 months) = 10% or sell at her *offer* of $\sigma_{implied}$(3 months) = 10.3%. Plugging $K = 1.37$, $S_t = 1.37$, and $\sigma_{implied}$(3 months) into $V_{BS}(S_t, t, \sigma_{implied}(T))$, in cash premium her bid is, say, 2.72 million USD and her offer is 2.81 million USD. Upon hearing these prices the customer decides that the option is cheap and wishes to buy.

However, during the period of enquiry, which typically lasts of the order of a few minutes, the price of EUR-USD spot drops to 1.3690. This drop is small, but it significantly changes the premium of the option. Recall from Chapter 2 that to first order the change in the price of the option is $\Delta(1.37, t, \phi) \times (1.37 - 1.3690) \times N$. Suppose that $\Delta(1.37, t, \phi) = 50\%$. Then off spot 1.3690, the trader will wish to adjust her bid and offer lower by 50 thousand USD to 2.67 million USD and 2.76 million USD respectively. By the time the market marker communicates the new price to the customer, spot may have moved yet again and changed the price yet again! However, in most circumstances, but by no means all, over a small spot move, the trader will be happy to still show the same $\sigma_{implied}(T)$ bid and offer. The customer therefore does not need to keep checking prices with the trader over a small range in spot because he can simply insert the quoted $\sigma_{implied}$(3 months) offer of 10.3% and the new value of S_t into $V_{BS}(S_t, t, \sigma_{implied}(T))$ to calculate the new price himself.

To summarize, the use of $\sigma_{implied}(T)$ means that option traders may extend prices to customers over small ranges in spot without having to continuously update the customer on the price. Even in the circumstance when the market maker wishes to adjust $\sigma_{implied}(T)$ in response to a movement in spot, the size and effect of this adjustment on the option premium is usually substantially smaller than that due to the spot move itself.

I hope that, given the discussion above, the reader is now able to understand Rebonato's apt description of $\sigma_{implied}(T)$ that I stated at the start of this chapter.

TRADING AN FX OPTION OVER THE COUNTER (OTC)—PART 2, DELTA EXCHANGE

A common method of executing an OTC option trade is to do so with *delta exchange*. In our example, the customer is buying the 3m EUR-USD $K = 1.37$ call option in 100 million EUR. At the time of the initial inquiry $S_t = 1.37$ and $\Delta_t = 50$ million EUR. The buyer of the option can agree to sell 50 million EUR to the seller of the option at 1.37, called the *spot reference*. Delta exchanges have at least two useful properties.

First, both parties in the transaction are costlessly delta hedged. Had the counterparties individually executed their delta hedges in the spot market, they would each likely have had to cross of the order of 1 pip on 50 million EUR = 5 thousand USD. This is ideal if both counterparties wish to expose themselves to volatility only.

Even if only the market maker wanted to delta hedge because the customer bought the option to express the joint view that EUR-USD spot would rise and volatility will be high, there is still a net cost saving to delta exchanging. The customer can delta exchange with the market maker and then purchase back 50 million EUR-USD in the spot market. Then, across the market maker and the customer only 50 million, rather than 100 million EUR-USD, are transacted in the spot market, costing of the order of 5 thousand, rather than 10 thousand USD.

Second, exchanging delta means that the premium also becomes insensitive to small changes in the spot rate. If spot moves from 1.37 to 1.3690, then the value of the option changes by approximately 50 thousand USD. However, this is also exactly the value of the delta

(Continued)

exchange. Therefore, both counterparties can continue to use 1.37 in the calculations without having to respond to each tick in the spot market.

The situation is more complicated if spot moves by a larger amount, for example, if spot moves from 1.37 to 1.36 and the counterparties agree to delta exchange using a spot reference of 1.37. The reason is that the option's gamma means that Δ_t for the option changes over the spot movement from 1.37 to 1.36. The value of the option diminishes by less than the gain of the delta hedge. There are also so-called *smile effects* that one must consider. I describe how the market maker should price the trade in these circumstances in Chapter 7.

6.2 TERM STRUCTURE

Term structure refers to $\sigma_{implied}(T)$ as a function of T. The term structure can be upward or downward sloping or non-monotonic. Further, the term structure moves multiple times each trading day. Options traders have developed a range of metrics that attempt to capture how the term structure may move, with the purpose of forecasting their PnL with respect to the day's movement. The three most commonly used metrics are *flat vega*, *weighted vega*, and *beta-weighted vega*.

However, it turns out that while these metrics are useful, they fail to capture significant parts of the movement in the term structure. To capture more, we must understand the main drivers. Some examples of these drivers are the current volatility environment, the market's perception of the long-run volatility environment, economic data releases, and political events, among others. Options traders have built models around these drivers. The remainder of this chapter is devoted to these ideas.

6.3 FLAT VEGA AND WEIGHTED VEGA GREEKS

Chapter 5 explained how to calculate the PnL implications associated with movements in $\sigma_{implied}(T)$. To briefly recapitulate, to first order, the trader must multiply her vega by the change in implied volatility. If she is using the change in $\sigma_{implied}(T)$, then she must multiply by $v_{BS}(S_t, t, \sigma_{implied}(T))$. She must use the change in $\sigma_{implied}(T)$ that corresponds to the T of the option in question.[1] If the trader holds a portfolio of options with multiple expiry times, then she must carry out this calculation corresponding to the T of each option.

However, there are strong relationships between $\sigma_{implied}(T)$ across T. For example, if $\sigma_{implied}(1m)$ rises, then most of the time $\sigma_{implied}(2m)$ will have risen also and so will other parts of the term structure. The central idea behind flat vega, weighted vega, and beta-weighted vega is to construct a single quantity that predicts the PnL of an option portfolio when $\sigma_{implied}(T)$ for a particular T changes. The trader may therefore divert her attention toward just one quantity and movements at one particular point of $\sigma_{implied}(T)$, say $\sigma_{implied}(1m)$.

6.3.1 Flat Vega

Flat vega assumes that $\sigma_{implied}(T)$ moves in parallel. So, if $\sigma_{implied}(1m)$ moves up by 1%, then so does $\sigma_{implied}(2m)$, $\sigma_{implied}(3m)$, and so forth. Flat vega is therefore calculated as

$$v_{BS}^{flat} = \sum_{i=1}^{k} v_{BS}^{i}(S_t, t, \sigma_{implied}(T_i)), \qquad (6.2)$$

where $v_{BS}^{i}(S_t, t, \sigma_{implied}(T))$ is the BSM vega of the ith option in a portfolio of k options and T_i denotes the expiry time of option i. If the trader believes that the term structure will move in a parallel manner, then she can multiply v_{BS}^{flat} by the amount that she expects the term structure to move.

Almost every options risk management software shows a flat vega number. This quantity is useful for several reasons. For example, following a new trade, the trader may wish to sanity check that her flat vega has changed by an amount equal to the vega on the new option she has dealt. However, as a risk management tool flat vega is of limited use. The reason is that parallel, or approximately parallel movements in the term structure are very rare.

In general, the short end, or front end, of the term structure, by which I mean $\sigma_{implied}(T)$ for small T, moves by a larger amount than the long end. Weighted vega is an attempt at capturing this.

---

[1]In the next chapter we see that she must multiply by the $\sigma_{implied}(T, K)$ that corresponds to the T and K of the option in question.

6.3.2 Weighted Vega

Weighted vega assumes that $\sigma_{implied}(T)$ moves in a square root manner. That is, if $\sigma_{implied}(1m)$ rises by x%, then the n month point rises by $\sqrt{\frac{1}{n}} \times x\%$. For example, if $\sigma_{implied}(1m)$ rises by 1%, then $\sigma_{implied}(6m)$ rises by 0.4%. Figure 6.2 illustrates both flat vega and weighted vega movements in $\sigma_{implied}(T)$.

For a portfolio of N options weighted vega is calculated as

$$v_{BS}^{wtd} = \sum_{i=1}^{k} \frac{1}{\sqrt{T_i - t}} v_{BS}^i (S_t, t, \sigma_{implied}(T_i)). \qquad (6.3)$$

Here, T_i is measured in months; a 1-month option will have $T - t = 1$. The claim is that if the $\sigma_{implied}(1m)$ point moves by x%, then the trader's PnL is given by $v_{BS}^{wtd} \times x$. There are at least three important points to note relating to flat vega, weighted vega, and their practical usage.

First, we understood from Chapter 5 that long expiry options and have more vega than short expiry options. Therefore, a portfolio constucted of largely longer expiry options will typically have more vega but less weighted vega than a similar sized portfolio consisting of shorter dated options. Some options traders therefore look at the difference between their v_{BS}^{flat} and v_{BS}^{wtd} as a measure of how short dated or long dated their overall portfolio is and use this difference as an additional risk management metric.

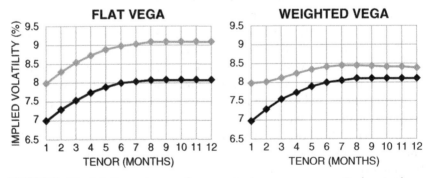

FIGURE 6.2 The left figure shows a flat move in the term structure. Each point has risen by 1%. The right figure shows a weighted move. The 1-month point has risen the most, by 1%, and the remainder of the term structure has risen proportional to the square root of the tenor.

Second, traders usually apply some form of bucketing and smoothing to calculate weighted vega rather than applying Equation (6.4) directly. By bucketing, I mean grouping options into a smaller number of tenors, called buckets. The following is an example of one of the most basic bucketing schemes.

Group every option that expires between 2 weeks and 6 weeks, sum their vegas, and put it into the 1-month bucket. Then, group every option with expiries between 6 weeks and 10 weeks, sum their vegas and put it into the 2-month bucket, and so forth across the tenor spectrum. Weighted vega is then calculated as

$$v_{BS}^{\text{wtd}} = \sum_{i=1}^{k} \frac{1}{\sqrt{i}} v_{BS}^{\text{bucket}}(i), \tag{6.4}$$

and flat vega as

$$v_{BS}^{\text{flat}} = \sum_{i=1}^{k} v_{BS}^{\text{bucket}}(i), \tag{6.5}$$

where $v_{BS}^{\text{bucket}}(i)$ is the vega in the i-month bucket and k is the number of buckets. For example, $k = 12$ if the trader's options all expire within 1 year or under and one uses a monthly bucketing scheme.

There are better bucketing schemes. For example, a 5-week option could have some weight fraction of its vega put into the 1-month bucket and the rest into the 2-month bucket. One can also optimize bucket granularity by using weekly buckets for shorter dated options and more coarse granularity, such as quarterly buckets, for longer expiry options. Here, I outline the practice only rather than describing bucketing in detail.

By smoothing, I mean that traders account for the fact that $1/(T-t)$ asymptotes as T gets small. A single very short-dated expiry option in the portfolio could therefore dominate the weighted vega calculation. Traders are aware that if $\sigma_{implied}(1m)$ moves by 1%, then $\sigma_{implied}(1\ \text{day})$ does not typically move by as much as $\sqrt{30} = 5.5\%$, although it is possible. They may smooth by removing the $1/(T-t)$ coefficient and setting it to, say 1 or another more appropriate fixed value, for $(T-t) < 1$ month.

Third, it is important to note the term stucture rarely, if ever, moves in a flat or weighted manner. This has led to attempts to design metrics that more accurately describe movements in the term structure than vega and weighted vega. The most intuitive is beta-weighted vega, which I discuss next.

6.3.3 Beta-Weighted Vega

The beta-weighted vega calculation is

$$v_{BS}^{beta} = \sum_{i=1}^{k} \beta_i v_{BS}^{bucket}(i). \tag{6.6}$$

Here, β_i are weights that are set by the trader often via an automated process. Note that weighted vega is a special case of beta-weighted vega with $\beta_i = 1/\sqrt{i}$ and flat vega is a special case with $\beta_i = 1$ and hence the beta-weighted vega method is a generalization.

A common process used to estimate β_i is to run the following regression for each value of i,

$$\sigma_{implied}(i)_t = \beta_i \sigma_{implied}(1m)_t + \varepsilon_t. \tag{6.7}$$

$\sigma_{implied}(i)_t$ and $\sigma_{implied}(1m)_t$ are the implied volatility of the i-month option and 1-month option respectively at time t and ε_t is a mean zero noise term. The regression can be run over a history or on a rolling basis using daily data.

The beta-weighted vega approach provides more flexibility than weighted vega or flat vega. However, even beta-weighted vega leaves significant movements in $\sigma_{implied}(T)$ unexplained for at least two reasons. First, the β_i are functions of time. A rolling regression attempts to capture this, but its backward-looking nature means that it is always, in effect, playing *catchup*. Second, the β_i are only ever estimates and are estimates of a model that may itself be severely misspecified.

Later in the chapter I describe a parameterized approach that captures almost all of the movement in $\sigma_{implied}(T)$. However, to understand this approach we must first understand the concept of forward volatility. This is the topic of the next section.

6.4 FORWARD VOLATILITY, FORWARD VARIANCE, AND TERM VOLATILITY

The log-return between time t and T is given by

$$\ln \frac{S_T}{S_t} = \ln \left(\frac{S_{t+1}}{S_t} \frac{S_{t+2}}{S_{t+1}} \frac{S_{t+3}}{S_{t+2}} \cdots \frac{S_T}{S_{T-1}} \right)$$

$$= \ln \frac{S_{t+1}}{S_t} + \ln \frac{S_{t+2}}{S_{t+1}} + \ln \frac{S_{t+3}}{S_{t+2}} + \ldots + \ln \frac{S_T}{S_{T-1}}.$$

Taking variances on both sides,

$$\sigma^2 \left(\ln \frac{S_T}{S_t} \right) = \sigma^2 \left(\ln \frac{S_{t+1}}{S_t} \right) + \sigma^2 \left(\ln \frac{S_{t+2}}{S_{t+1}} \right) + \ldots + \sigma^2 \left(\ln \frac{S_T}{S_{T-1}} \right). \quad (6.8)$$

Here, I make the important assumption that spot returns are not auto-correlated. Otherwise, covariance terms would appear on the right-hand side in the equation above. For interested readers, I provide empirical evidence supporting this assumption in Chapter 11.

The terms $\sigma^2(\ln(S_{t+i+1}/S_{t+i}))$ are called *forward variances*, because they refer to the variance of the log spot return over the period of time in the future, $t + i$ to $t + i + 1$.

To understand the relationship between forward variance and forward volatility, let us take as an example the case where we measure time in months and set $T = 3$. In words, Equation (6.8) tells us that the variance of the log spot return over the next three months is given by the sum of the variances over the first month and the forward variances over months 2 and 3. Suppose, for example, that the implied variance in month 1 is 10 units, the implied forward variance in month 2 is 12 units, and the implied forward variance in month 3 is 14 units:

$$\underbrace{\sigma^2 \left(\ln \frac{S_{3\text{mth}}}{S_t} \right)}_{\text{36 units of variance}} = \underbrace{\sigma^2 \left(\ln \frac{S_{1\text{mth}}}{S_t} \right)}_{\text{10 units of variance}} + \underbrace{\sigma^2 \left(\ln \frac{S_{2\text{mth}}}{S_{1\text{mth}}} \right)}_{\text{12 units of forward variance}}$$

$$+ \underbrace{\sigma^2 \left(\ln \frac{S_{3\text{mth}}}{S_{2\text{mth}}} \right)}_{\text{14 units of forward variance}} .$$

The total implied variance over 3 months is 36 units. The standard deviation is the square root of the variance and therefore the 3-month implied standard deviation is 6. However, recall that σ_i and $\sigma_{implied}$ are annualized quantities and I therefore note than the 3-month annualized standard devation is 6% $\times$ $\sqrt{12/3} = 12\%$.

Next, let us calculate the forward volatilities. I denote the forward implied volatility from month n to month m by $\sigma_i(n \to m)$.

The 1-month implied volatility is straightforward. There are 10 units of implied variance between t and 1 month. The implied volatility is therefore $\sqrt{10} = 3.16$. Annualizing this gives us $\sigma_i(1 \text{ month}) = 3.12 \times \sqrt{12/1} = 10.95\%$.

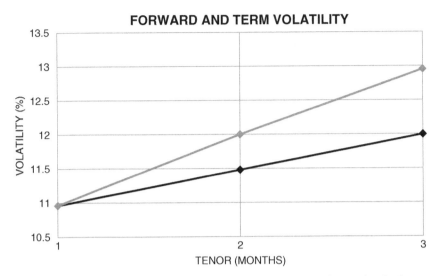

FIGURE 6.3 The light gray line shows the term structure of the forward volatility and the black line shows the term structure of term volatility. The light gray line is upward sloping, meaning that the market expects each month to be more volatile than the previous month. The black line is therefore correspondingly upward sloping.

The 1-month → 2-month forward implied volatility (also described as the 1-month in 1-month implied volatility) is $\sqrt{12} = 3.46$. This gives us $\sigma_i(1\text{m} \to 2\text{m}) = 3.46 \times \sqrt{12/1} = 12\%$. The 2-month volatility is $\sqrt{22} = 4.69$. Annualizing this gives us the 2-month term volatility, $\sigma_i(2 \text{ month}) = 4.69 \times \sqrt{12/2} = 11.48\%$.

The 2-month → 3-month forward implied volatility (also described as the 1-month in 2-month implied volatility) is $\sqrt{14} = 3.74$. This gives us $\sigma_i(2\text{m} \to 3\text{m}) = 3.74 \times \sqrt{12/1} = 12.96\%$.

Figure 6.3 plots $\sigma_i(T)$ and the forward implied volatilities corresponding to this example.

6.4.1 Calculating Implied Forward Volatility

Options traders quote and trade term volatilities. At this point, traders typically assume that the log-normal distribution and hence the BSM approach holds and let $\sigma_{implied}$ denote the annualized standard deviation of the PDF. The reason that they are happy to do so is that they then re-input smile as described in Chapters 7 and 8 so that options are priced with a non-log-normal PDF once again. I therefore continue to make the log-normal assumption over the rest of this chapter and return to the subtleties mentioned here in the next chapter.

Market participants imply forward volatilities from term volatilities. Here, I derive an equation to do so. Suppose that we wish to calculate $\sigma_{implied}(n \to m)$. Equation (6.8) tells us that

$$\sigma^2\left(\frac{S_{t+m}}{S_{t+n}}\right) = \sigma^2\left(\frac{S_{t+m}}{S_t}\right) - \sigma^2\left(\frac{S_{t+n}}{S_t}\right).$$

Annualizing and dropping the difference between $\sigma_{implied}$ and the annualized standard deviation then gives us

$$\sigma_{implied}(n \to m)^2\left(\frac{m-n}{\alpha}\right) = \sigma_{implied}(m)^2\left(\frac{m}{\alpha}\right) - \sigma^2_{implied}\left(\frac{n}{\alpha}\right).$$

Above, α cancels out, but I include it to make the annualization method clear. If m and n are measured in months, then $\alpha = 12$. If m and n are measured in days, then $\alpha = 365$, and so forth. Finally, rearranging gives us our formula for forward implied volatility,

$$\sigma_{implied}(n \to m) = \sqrt{\frac{m\sigma^2_{implied}(m) - n\sigma^2_{implied}(n)}{m - n}}. \tag{6.9}$$

Options traders should commit this formula to memory.

6.5   BUILDING A TERM STRUCTURE MODEL USING DAILY FORWARD VOLATILITY

Market participants can trade options expiring on any business day. Options traders therefore typically use increments of one day in Equation (6.8). They then assign a volatility to each individual day. Figure 6.4 provides some insight into how an option trader may construct the term structure.

The first column in Figure 6.4 shows the date. The typical date range in this setup is one or two years. For longer expiry options the detail of each individual trading day becomes less relevant and traders tend to use a more coarse approach. Note that the dates include weekends. The reason is that FX options use 365 days in their annualization.

| Term Structure Builder | | | | | |
Date	Base Vol	Event Vol	Fwd Vol	Notes	Expiry Vol
03-Oct-17	7.95%		7.95%		7.95%
04-Oct-17	8.00%		8.00%		7.98%
05-Oct-17	8.05%		8.05%		8.00%
06-Oct-17	8.10%	3.00%	11.10%	Non Farm Payrolls	8.88%
07-Oct-17	8.20%	−8.20%	0.00%	Weekend	7.94%
08-Oct-17	8.25%	−8.25%	0.00%	Weekend	7.25%
09-Oct-17	8.30%		8.30%		7.41%
10-Oct-17	8.35%		8.35%		7.53%
11-Oct-17	8.40%		8.40%		7.63%
12-Oct-17	8.43%		8.43%		7.72%

FIGURE 6.4 The figure shows a common method used to build $\sigma_{implied}(T)$. Many options traders use a setup of this nature to price options expiries of up to two years.

The second column shows *base volatility*. The idea is to specify a forecast of annualized volatility over each 24-hour forward period if the date in question were a normal business day. I discuss how the trader may look to do this in the next section. Here, I have shown an upward-sloping term structure of base volatility.

The third column shows *event volatility*. This column adds or subtracts volatility depending on the nature of the day in question. In the example, 6-Oct-17 has 3.00% extra volatility due to the fact that non-farm payroll data is released on that Friday. The next day, 7-Oct-17, has −8.20% due to it being a Saturday. The relevant information is displayed in the *notes* column.

The fourth column is *forward volatility*. This sums the base volatility and event volatility.

Finally, the fifth column shows *expiry volatility*. Expiry volatility is calculated by applyng Equation (6.8) to the forward volatility column. For example, to calculate the Expiry Vol for, say 6-Oct-17, the calculation is $\frac{1}{4}(7.95\%^2 + 8.00\%^2 + 8.05\%^2 + 11.10\%^2) = 8.88\%$.

Options market makers spend substantial effort manipulating the numbers in tables such as Figure 6.4. The method allows option traders to consistently price volatility across every trading day. For example, the amount of variance priced into a 9-day option will be consistent with the amount of variance priced into the first 9 days of a 10-day expiry option.

This method also ensures consistency across time. For example, after a day goes past, the first row will be deleted, and all future days will again be priced in a time consistent manner.

Sanity Checking Forward Volatilities Note that the quantities in the forward volatility column in Figure 6.4 are 1-day forward volatilities. The trader may therefore apply the formula given in Equation (1.3) to approximate the breakeven anticipated for the 1-day ATMS straddle over each of the days listed. For example, the forward volatility for 6-Oct-17 is 11.10%. Therefore, the breakeven is $\pm 0.47\%$. A movement in EUR-USD spot of this magnitude on the release of payrolls data sounds intuitively reasonable based on historic data and experience.

In the feature box I show that the implied probability that S_T exceeds the breakeven is 42% in the context of a normal model, and that this quantity is independent of the implied volatility. Therefore, the trader may confirm that the breakeven of $\pm 0.47\%$ sounds reasonable if she thinks that the probability that it is exceeded is around 42%. In Chapter 9 I show that this result is also approximately true in the log-normal context.

PROBABILITY OF EXCEEDING THE BREAKEVEN

I continue from the feature box on page 63. First,

$$S_T \sim \mathcal{N}(S_t, \sigma_n^2)$$

The probability that $S_T - S_t$ is larger than the breakeven is given by

$$2 \times \text{Prob}_t\left(\frac{S_T - S_t}{\sigma_n} > \frac{4.2\sigma_i\sqrt{n}S_t}{100\sigma_n}\right) = 2\left[1 - N\left(\frac{4.2\sqrt{365}}{100}\right)\right]$$
$$= 42\%. \qquad (6.10)$$

In the first line I use Equation (3.12) for the breakeven. I also use $\sigma_n = \sqrt{\frac{n}{365}}\sigma_i S_t$ as on page 63. The multiplicative factor of 2 comes from the fact that the breakeven can be exceeded by spot moving higher or lower.

6.6   SETTING BASE VOLATILITY USING A THREE-PARAMETER GARCH MODEL

Setting base volatility for two years of individual days is inconvenient. It is also clear that there should be relationships between the individual days. For example, if one's forecast of base volatility on day x rises, then one expects that their forecast for day $x + 1$ will be higher also. One way to capture these relationships is to use a volatility forecasting model. This has the effect of decreasing the number of parameters that need to be set from 730 to the number of parameters in the model. Here, I introduce the so-called GARCH(1,1)[2] 3-parameter model.

GARCH is a volatility forecasting model introduced by Bollerslev (1986), who generalized the seminal ARCH approach of Engle (1982). The idea behind GARCH is to capture two features of empirical volatility data. The first is that volatility is autoregressive, meaning that periods of high (low) volatility are often followed by periods of high (low) volatility. The second is that volatility is mean reverting. The next feature box discusses the GARCH model in more detail. Here, I provide the main result that is used in practical options trading.

GARCH tells us that

$$\mathbb{E}_t[\sigma_{t+i}^2] = \sigma_{final}^2 + e^{-i\frac{\ln 2}{H}}(\sigma_t^2 - \sigma_{final}^2).\qquad(6.11)$$

Let us understand each of the terms in turn.

Using daily returns, σ_{t+i}^2 is the variance of the one-day log spot return i days from today. Traders interpret the square root of $\mathbb{E}_t[\sigma_{t+i}^2]$ as base volatility because this quantity is the forecast, or expectation, of the variance that will occur i days from today, without adjusting for economic events. If $i = 0$, then $\mathbb{E}_t[\sigma_t^2] = \sigma_t^2$ as expected. σ_t is the volatility occurring on the present day. This is the first of the three parameters set by the options trader.

Next, let $i \to \infty$. Then $\mathbb{E}_t[\sigma_\infty^2] = \sigma_{final}^2$. σ_{final}^2 is the expectation of the long-run forward variance, or terminal variance. It is analogous to the terminal rate used in fixed income trading. Again, this is a parameter set by the options trader.

---

[2]GARCH is an acronym for Generalized Autoregressive Conditional Heteroskedasticity.

The third parameter is H, or half life. It is measured in days. To understand this, set $i = H$. Then

$$\mathbb{E}_t[\sigma_{t+H}^2] = \sigma_t^2 + \frac{1}{2}(\sigma_{final}^2 - \sigma_t^2),$$

so that, after H days, our forecast of the variance is halfway between its present value σ_t^2 and its long-run value σ_{final}^2.

The GARCH approach is able to generate monotonic upward or downward term structures of base volatility. If the current economic environment is more volatile than the unconditional average, $\sigma_t > \sigma_{final}$, then the term structure of base volatility is downward sloping. The opposite is true if $\sigma_t < \sigma_{final}$. The base forward volatilities always tends toward, but never reaches, σ_{final}.

The reader should note that using the GARCH model does not imply that the term structure of implied volatility is always monotonic. The reason is that we have not yet added economic events. For instance, if there is a significant economic event within 1 month, then we may still have $\sigma_{implied}(1 \text{ month}) > \sigma_{implied}(2 \text{ month})$ even with $\sigma_t < \sigma_{final}$.

GENERALIZED AUTROREGRESSIVE CONDITIONAL HETEROSKEDASTICITY (GARCH)

The most commonly used version of GARCH is the so-called GARCH(1,1) model. It says that the daily variance follows

$$\sigma_{t+1}^2 = \omega + \beta \sigma_t^2 + \alpha r_t^2. \tag{6.12}$$

Here, ω, α, and β are constants, r_t is the log-return from time $t - 1$ to t, and $\mathbb{E}_t[r^2] = \sigma_t^2$. That is, the variance tomorrow σ_{t+1}^2 is determined by the variance that was forecast for today, the return that occurred today, and the coefficients ω, α, and β.

Taking the conditional expectation on both sides of Equation (6.12),

$$\mathbb{E}_t[\sigma_{t+1}^2] = \omega + (\alpha + \beta)\sigma_t^2.$$

(Continued)

Taking the unconditional expectation,

$$\mathbb{E}[\sigma_{t+1}^2] = \omega + (\alpha + \beta)\mathbb{E}[\sigma_t^2]$$

$$\implies \mathbb{E}[\sigma_t^2] = \frac{\omega}{1 - \alpha - \beta}, \qquad (6.13)$$

because $\mathbb{E}[\sigma_{t+1}^2] = \mathbb{E}[\sigma_t^2]$. We require $\alpha + \beta < 1$ for this quantity to be defined. After some basic algebraic manipulation,

$$\mathbb{E}_t[\sigma_{t+1}^2] - \frac{\omega}{1 - \alpha - \beta} = (\alpha + \beta)\left(\sigma_t^2 - \frac{\omega}{1 - \alpha - \beta}\right).$$

Therefore

$$\mathbb{E}_t[\sigma_{t+i}^2] = \frac{\omega}{1 - \alpha - \beta} + (\alpha + \beta)^i \left(\sigma_t^2 - \frac{\omega}{1 - \alpha - \beta}\right)$$

$$= \sigma_{final}^2 + e^{\frac{-i\ln 2}{H}}(\sigma_t^2 - \sigma_{final}^2),$$

where $\sigma_{final}^2 = \frac{\omega}{1-\alpha-\beta}$ and $H = \frac{-\ln 2}{\ln(\alpha+\beta)}$. This is the three-parameter model in Equation (6.11).

6.6.1 Applying the Three-Parameter Model

Figure 6.5 plots the base vol and shows a snippet of the term structure builder for a sample set of parameters.

In practice the parameters are set by marking to market. If the options trader were to raise σ_t, then this raises the short end of $\sigma_{implied}(T)$ more than the long end. Similarly, raising σ_{final} raises the long end more than the short end. Adjusting H changes the steepness of the slope. Raising H means that the day that the forecast of forward variance reaches halfway between σ_t and σ_{final} is further away, and therefore the slope is flatter. The trader adjusts the parameters until her $\sigma_{implied}(T)$ best fits the market.

Note that traders observe expiry volatility, which contains both base volatility and event volatility. Therefore, marking the parameters to market must be carried out as a joint exercise with setting event volatility. I discuss setting event volatility later in the chapter.

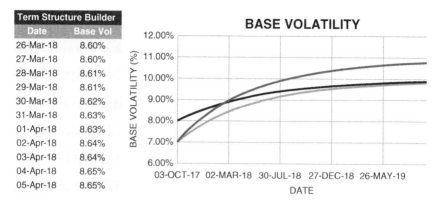

Term Structure Builder	
Date	Base Vol
26-Mar-18	8.60%
27-Mar-18	8.60%
28-Mar-18	8.61%
29-Mar-18	8.61%
30-Mar-18	8.62%
31-Mar-18	8.63%
01-Apr-18	8.63%
02-Apr-18	8.64%
03-Apr-18	8.64%
04-Apr-18	8.65%
05-Apr-18	8.65%

FIGURE 6.5 The chart shows the term structure of base volatility for three sets of parameters. The light gray line uses $\sigma_t = 7.00\%$, $\sigma_{final} = 10\%$ and $H = 180$ days. The black line keeps σ_{final} and H unchanged, but raises σ_t to 8%. The dark gray line keeps σ_t and H unchanged but raises σ_{final} to 11%. The table on the left shows the forward variance reaching halfway between $\sigma_t^2 = 7.00\%^2$ and $\sigma_{final}^2 = 10.0\%^2$ after 180 days.

6.6.2 Limitations of GARCH

The GARCH model works well in practical market making. However, there are at least two major limitations. The first relates to the very long end of the term structure. One is not usually able to calibrate the GARCH model parameters to fit the term structure beyond the 2-year point in a manner that is consistent with the term structure up until the 2-year point.

There are several reasons that one can speculate upon to explain this. First, the GARCH model may be misspecified and additional parameters may be required. For instant, interest rate effects may become more significant at the long end of the curve, and such effects must be built on top of the GARCH model.

Second, there may be market segmentation. If different participants trade the long end of the curve compared with the short end of the curve, and few participants have the capacity to hold option positions the many years that are required to exploit the inconsistencies, there is no relative value reason that the long end of the curve and short end of the curve are forced to be consistent with one another; there is nobody to take advantage of mispricing.

The second limitation of the GARCH approach is at the very short end of the term structure. Traders often add additional parameters over and above the GARCH model to account for very short-term spikes and troughs in realized volatility. I leave this topic for future discussion.

6.6.3 Risk Management Using the Three-Parameter Model

Instead of vega, weighted vega, or beta-weighted vega, a trader using the GARCH approach may employ three metrics. They are

$$v^{\sigma_t} = \sum_{i=1}^{k} \frac{\partial \sigma_{implied}(i)}{\partial \sigma_t} v_{BS}^{bucket}(i), \tag{6.14}$$

$$v^{\sigma_{final}} = \sum_{i=1}^{k} \frac{\partial \sigma_{implied}(i)}{\partial \sigma_{final}} v_{BS}^{bucket}(i), \tag{6.15}$$

$$v^{H} = \sum_{i=1}^{k} \frac{\partial \sigma_{implied}(i)}{\partial H} v_{BS}^{bucket}(i). \tag{6.16}$$

These metrics quantify a portfolio's exposure to the three parameters in the GARCH model. Since the GARCH model fits the term structure of implied volatility well at all times in practice, up to the limitations already discussed above, σ_t, σ_{final}, and H capture much of the variation in the base volatility and substantially more so than v_{BS}^{flat}, v_{BS}^{wtd}, and v_{BS}^{beta}. Therefore, a hedging options trader acting to minimize her exposure to v^{σ_t}, $v^{\sigma_{final}}$, and v^{H} should experience less PnL variance than one looking to minimize any of v_{BS}^{flat}, v_{BS}^{wtd}, and v_{BS}^{beta}, all else being equal.

6.6.4 Empirical GARCH Estimation

One may suggest empirically estimating the GARCH model using historic data in order to set the parameters. However, options traders rarely do this for at least two reasons. First, note that the GARCH model is used to set base volatility only. Historic data contains returns that have taken place over events.

Second, even if the econometrician were to construct an appropriate filtering scheme for economic events, there remains the issue of risk premiums. Although I have not discussed risk premiums in detail in this text, it is worth noting that the estimated parameters would be based on historic data, whereas the parameters that fit the market contain a volatility risk premium.

For instance, σ_{final} implied by option prices in the market is higher than its empirical estimate. This is the well-documented *volatility risk premium*.

6.7 VOLATILITY CARRY AND FORWARD VOLATILITY AGREEMENTS

Suppose that $\sigma_{implied}(T)$ is upward sloping. Based on the analysis of forward volatility gained in Section 6.4, we understand that this means that the market is pricing volatility to rise in the future. Loosely put, a *volatility carry* strategy speculates that the shape of the term structure will remain unchanged over a period of time so that volatility will not rise as forecast, or it will rise by less than forecast. The strategy is perhaps best understood via an example. Here, I provide a simple example via a contract known as a forward volatility agreement (FVA).

Let $\sigma_{implied}(3 \text{ month}) = 8\%$, $\sigma_{implied}(6 \text{ month}) = 8.25\%$, $\sigma_{implied}(9 \text{ month})$ $= 8.5\%$, and $\sigma_{implied}(1 \text{ year}) = 8.75\%$. Applying Equation (6.9) we calculate that the forward implied volatilities over each 3-month period are $\sigma_{implied}(3m \to 6m) = 8.49\%$, $\sigma_{implied}(6m \to 9m) = 8.98\%$, and $\sigma_{implied}$ $(9m \to 1y) = 9.46\%$.

The trader enters into a 3-month in 9-month short FVA position. This means that she agrees to sell a 3m ATM straddle in 9 months' time at a price that is specified today. The current value of $\sigma_{implied}(9m \to 1y)$ is 9.46% and this is the price that she agrees to sell at. She therefore profits if, in 9 months' time, $\sigma_{implied}(3 \text{ month}) < 9.46\%$. She chooses a notional of 100 million EUR per leg of the straddle.

The FVA is priced higher than the current 3-month contract because the market expects volatility to increase in the future. If volatility does not increase over the next 9 months, or if it increases by less than is forecast, then the short FVA position profits.

Suppose that $\sigma_{implied}(T)$ remains unchanged over the 9-month period and that the trader has successfully volatility carry traded. Her mark-to-market profit can be calculated using vega. Applying Equation (5.3) to a 3-month option we calculate her profit as $v_{BS} \times [\sigma_{implied}(9m \to 1y) - \sigma_{implied}(3 \text{ month})] = \frac{4.2}{100} \times \sqrt{91} \times 100$ million EUR $\times (9.46\% - 8\%) = 585$ thousand EUR.

The trader does not need to wait a full 9 months in order to profit. For example, she can wait just 3 months. Again, if $\sigma_{implied}(T)$ remains unchanged, then since the price of the 3-month in 6-month FVA is

$\sigma_{implied}(6m \rightarrow 9m) = 8.98\%$, she profits by unwinding her trade. In this case her profit is $v_{BS} \times [\sigma_{implied}(9m \rightarrow 1y) - \sigma_{implied}(6m \rightarrow 9m)] = \frac{4.2}{100} \times \sqrt{91} \times$ 100 million EUR $\times (9.46\% - 8.98\%) = 192$ thousand EUR. For simplicity, the calculations here do not account for transaction costs.

Taking this idea further, the trader may look to optimize the strategy by finding the *steepest* part of the term structure to allow her to sell optionality and buy it back at a lower price in the shortest time available. Indeed, many options traders have spent effort in locating the steepest parts of the term structure.

The GARCH model provides some much-needed clarity on this topic. It provides the elegant result that much of this effort is wasted, and that no part of the term structure is a better sell than any other part. This is the topic of the next subsection.

6.7.1   Volatility Carry in the GARCH Model

In the GARCH model, σ_t is forecast to move toward σ_{final} each day. Applying Equation (6.11) the size of this movement is calculated as

$$\sqrt{\mathbb{E}[\sigma_{t+1}^2]} - \sigma_t = \sqrt{\sigma_{final}^2 + e^{-\frac{\ln 2}{H}}(\sigma_t^2 - \sigma_{final}^2)} - \sigma_t. \qquad (6.17)$$

If the volatility carry strategy is successful, and the term structure remains unchanged, then all that has happened from the perspective of the GARCH model is that σ_t was forecast to rise by the amount calculated in Equation (6.17), but it did not. The component of the trader's PnL that can be attributed to volatility carry over the 24-hour period is then simply

$$\text{Overnight Carry} = -\left(\sqrt{\mathbb{E}[\sigma_{t+1}^2]} - \sigma_t\right) \times v^{\sigma_t}. \qquad (6.18)$$

This equation is particularly interesting because it shows that carry depends on only two components. The first is the rate that volatility is expected to rise, as determined by the parameters of the GARCH model that are calibrated to market. The second is the trader's portfolio's exposure to σ_t. The important point to note is that v^{σ_t} can arise from options of any tenor. One can sell a 1-month option to generate an exposure of say, −100 thousand USD, or an amount of a 6-month option to generate the same exposure.

The key insight is this: In the context of GARCH, effort spent on locating steep and flat parts of the term structure to construct carry strategies is largely wasted.

6.7.2 Common Pitfalls in Volatility Carry Trading

$\sigma_{implied}(T)$ can often appear to have strange shapes. It may contain apparent dips that suggest buying opportunities, or peaks that look like selling opportunities. On occasion they may be, but more often than not, a GARCH approach to base volatility with economic events, weekends, and holidays overlayed as described in Section 6.5 provides clarity to the term structure and shows that it is internally self consistent by construction.

Here, I do not argue that carry strategies are not viable. One may disagree with the GARCH formulation and believe that the term structure of base volatility should be non-monotonic, for example. I argue only that the GARCH construction highlights the possibility that it is easy to waste effort on carry strategies.

Finally, note here that assessing volatility overlays for economic events, weekends, and holidays can add efficacy to a volatility carry strategy.

6.8 TRADER'S SUMMARY

- $\sigma_{implied}(T)$ is the number that one must plug into the BSM formula to calculate the premium of an option. Options market participants have agreed on this use.
- Using $\sigma_{implied}(T)$ and the BSM formula is useful because it allows traders to quote prices in terms of $\sigma_{implied}(T)$, which moves more slowly than the option premium.
- Most movements in the option premium are driven by movements in spot. Traders often delta exchange to mitigate this. Delta exchange is effective over small movements in spot and it can lead to cost savings.
- The term structure refers to how $\sigma_{implied}(T)$ varies as a function of T. Traders make assumptions on how $\sigma_{implied}(T)$ can move over time and calculate metrics to quantify their PnL risk to these movements, namely flat vega, weighted vega, and beta-weighted vega.
- Flat vega is the PnL to a flat move in $\sigma_{implied}(T)$ across T.
- Weighted vega is the PnL to move in $\sigma_{implied}(T)$ where each point moves proportional to the square root of T.
- Beta-weighted vega is the PnL to move in $\sigma_{implied}(T)$ where each point moves based on an empirically estimated β.
- Traders typically build $\sigma_{implied}(T)$ using a day-by-day model. Each day is assigned a forward volatility that is composed of a base volatility and an event volatility.

- The base volatility is often set using a parameterized model. GARCH(1,1) is a suitable 3-parameter model. However, traders more commonly use a 5-parameter model, using the two additional parameters to capture movements at the short end of the term structure.
- Expectations of future volatility can be calculated using Equation (6.17). Volatility carry is a strategy that exploits the idea that these expectations may differ from future realizations.
- The GARCH approach makes clear that volatility carry strategies can be constructed using any part of the term structure. It is not clear that effort spent locating steepness is necessarily fruitful.

CHAPTER **7**

Vanna, Risk Reversal, and Skewness

In the previous chapter I discussed that traders use the BSM function to value options by defining $\sigma_{implied}$ such that $V_t = V_{BS}(S_t, t, \sigma_{implied}, K)$. This chapter focuses on a serious shortcoming of this approach; it is not in general possible to use the same value of $\sigma_{implied}$ to price options of two different strikes on a particular expiry date.

Traders adjust for this shortcoming using *smile*. Smile refers to the fact that the value of $\sigma_{implied}$ that must be inserted into V_{BS} to match the prices of traded options is not constant across different strikes. For example, a 1-year expiry OTM put may trade with a higher $\sigma_{implied}$ than the ATM strike. That is, $\sigma_{implied}$ is made a function of strike and one must write $\sigma_{implied}(K)$. The function $\sigma_{implied}(K)$ happens to look like a smile, as we will see ahead.

There are two main reasons for the existence of smile relating to the PDF of log spot returns. The first is skewness; historic realizations of the spot PDF are asymmetric, giving OTM puts and calls different values of $\sigma_{implied}$. The BSM approach assumed that log returns are symmetric and hence V_{BS} was never designed to capture the asymmetry. Figure 7.3 shows a skewed PDF and a normal PDF overlayed.

The second is kurtosis; historic realizations of the spot PDF have fatter tails than implied by the log-normal, giving OTM options higher values than ATM options relative to those implied by the BSM function and a constant $\sigma_{implied}$. I discuss skewness in this chapter and kurtosis in Chapter 8.

Skewness is related to two other concepts in options, namely vanna and risk reversal. Let us understand these ideas and how they are related to each other.

Vanna Vanna describes how the vega $v(S_t, t, \phi)$ of an option varies with spot. It is defined as,

$$\text{Vanna} \equiv \frac{\partial v(S_t, t, \sigma_i)}{\partial S} = \frac{\partial \Delta(S_t, t, \sigma_i)}{\partial \sigma_i}. \qquad (7.1)$$

The second equality tells us that vanna also describes how $\Delta(S_t, t, \sigma_i)$ varies with σ_i.[1] If vanna > 0 so that the trader is *long vanna*, then $v(S_t, t, \sigma_i)$ rises when spot S_t rises, and $\Delta(S_t, t, \sigma_i)$ rises if σ_i rises. Therefore, a trader holding a long vanna position will root for σ_i to rise when S_t rises. I discuss this idea in more detail later in the chapter but note at this stage that the correlation between S_t and σ_i, commonly refered to as *spot-vol correlation*, plays an important role. A trader holding a long vanna position benefits from positive realizations of spot-vol correlation.

The previous chapter discussed the vega profile of a single option. By combining multiple options with different strikes together traders can create more complex vega profiles. A typical options portfolio can contain anything from a few to a few thousand options. In order to understand how the vega of such a portfolio behaves in aggregation as S_t moves, traders turn to vanna because it amalgamates all of this information into a single number.

Risk Reversal The term *risk reversal* has two meanings. Its most basic meaning refers to a payoff structure. It is an option structure that consists of purchasing an OTM call option and selling an OTM put option (or vice versa). Its payoff diagram is shown in Figure 7.1.

One can immediately see how the risk reversal and vanna relate to each other. If the trader purchases the OTM call and sells the OTM put, she benefits from positive spot-vol correlation because as S_t moves toward her long strike and away from her short strike σ_i is expected to rise and so does $v(S_t, t, \sigma_i)$. The risk reversal is the most common option structure that traders use to provide exposure to vanna while not adding significantly to their other exposures, such as vega and gamma.

In real markets traders expect certain spot-vol correlations to hold. For example, during economic crises investors demand safe haven currencies such as JPY, and sell currencies perceived as more risky, such as AUD. Crises are also a time of rising σ_i. Therefore, currency pairs such as AUD-JPY depreciate and the spot-vol correlation performs negatively. In the risk reversal

---

[1]To see this simply swap the order of the partial derivatives: $\frac{\partial v}{\partial S} = \frac{\partial}{\partial S} \frac{\partial V}{\partial \sigma} = \frac{\partial}{\partial \sigma} \frac{\partial V}{\partial S} = \frac{\partial \Delta}{\partial \sigma}$.

structure, therefore, traders typically price the OTM put at a higher price than the OTM call, thereby accounting for the expected negative correlation. The difference in $\sigma_{implied}(K)$ between the equivalent OTM call and OTM put is also known as the risk reversal and this is second meaning of the term *risk reversal*. I explain these ideas in more detail ahead.

7.1   RISK REVERSAL

A risk reversal consists of either buying an OTM call option and selling an OTM put option, or vice versa. Figure 7.1 shows the payoff and vega profile of this strategy.

In Figure 7.1 the trader has purchased the EUR call and sold the EUR put. The vega profile shows that her portfolio is flat vega when spot is at its starting point 1.37. However, if spot rises, then she *derives* longer vega. This continues until a peak, which exists either at or beyond the strike of the call option. Similarly, she derives shorter vega as spot falls. This continues until a trough, which exists either at or below the strike of the put option. The trader is long vanna as long as spot is between the strike of the put and the strike of the call.

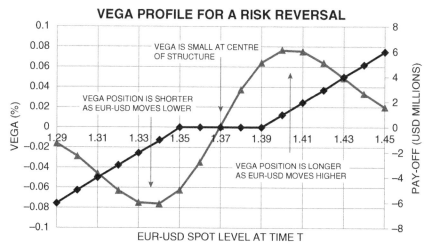

FIGURE 7.1   The figure shows the vega profile of a 1-month expiry risk reversal structure consisting of the purchase of a EUR-USD call option with $K = 1.39$ and sale of a put with $K = 1.35$. With EUR-USD spot at 1.37 the strikes of the call and put are equidistant and so the vega of the structure is close to zero. However, if spot rises (falls), the position derives longer (shorter) vega. Note that the peak points in vega occur when EUR-USD is beyond the call strike or the put strike.

Suppose that there is a correlation between spot and σ_i in that when EUR-USD moves lower, σ_i rises (negative spot-vol correlation). For example, if the probability of a Eurozone crisis rose, then one may expect EUR-USD spot to fall and the demand for options, and hence σ_i to rise. If this happened, then the trader's position of long the call and short the put would perform poorly. The trader needs to be compensated to take on this risk. She is compensated because the market will price the put at a higher price than the *equivalent* call when it expects negative spot-vol correlation. I explain my use of the term *equivalent* in more detail in Section 7.3. For now, the reader may understand it very approximately as a call option with strike a similar distance above S_t as the put option has strike below S_t.

The way that the market prices the put higher than the call is by making $\sigma_{implied}$ itself a function of strike K, $\sigma_{implied}(K)$. In this example, if K is lower than S_t, $\sigma_{implied}(K)$ is higher, and if K is higher than S_t, then $\sigma_{implied}(K)$ is lower. Figure 7.2 shows this graphically. This function is called a volatility *smile*.

The example in Figure 7.1 shows a 1-month expiry 1.35 versus 1.39 risk reversal. The price of the structure is calculated as follows. Reading off

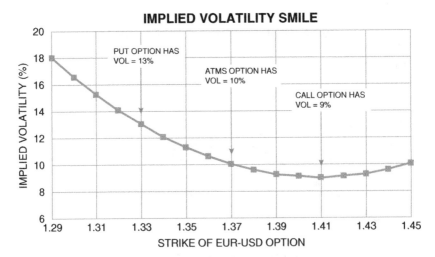

FIGURE 7.2 The figure shows an implied volatility smile, $\sigma_{implied}(K)$. In this example, the call option trades at a lower value of $\sigma_{implied}$ than the put option. That is, $\sigma_{implied}(1.41) < \sigma_{implied}(1.33)$. If the smile takes this shape, the market is telling us that σ_i is expected to rise if EUR-USD falls and fall if EUR-USD rises. There is an expectation of negative spot-vol correlation.

Figure 7.2, we can see that $\sigma_{implied}(1.35) = 11.5\%$. Plug this into the BSM formula to calculate the premium of the put. Similarly, plug $\sigma_{implied}(1.39) = 9.25\%$ into the BSM formula to calculate the premium of the call. Although I have not yet introduced the BSM formula, other than for an ATM option (I do so in Chapter 10) we can intuit at this stage that plugging in a higher (lower $\sigma_{implied}$) raises (lowers) the resulting premium.

Finally, note that in FX markets, the volatility smile is typically constructed in *delta space*. Briefly, this means that traders set $\sigma_{implied}(\Delta)$, $\sigma_{implied}$ as a function of Δ, rather than as a function of K. I explain this in more detail in Section 7.3.

7.2 SKEWNESS

So far I have discussed vanna and risk reversals as providing exposure to spot-vol correlation. In this section I show that spot-vol correlation is analogous to skewness in the spot PDF.

Figure 7.3 shows a negatively skewed PDF (black) and a symmetric PDF (light gray). There are two main features to note.

First, the distribution is asymmetric in that there is a long left tail (there is a probabilty of a fast devaluation in the spot rate), but the right tail is shorter than that of the normal. Intuitively, this ties out with the idea of negative spot-vol correlation. If σ_i falls when spot rises, then this may cause spot to remain bound and so the right tail is short. The opposite is true at the left tail. I further explain this idea later.

Second, the peak of the distribution has shifted to the right. This means that spot is more likely to go up than down, but if it goes down, the move is larger. Note that this does not violate our key equation, $S_t = \mathbb{E}[S_T]$, that says that the expected change in spot is zero. Recall I provided an example to illustrate this non-violation in Section 2.7.

More formally, skewness is defined as

$$\text{Skew} = \mathbb{E}\left[\frac{r^3}{\sigma^3}\right], \tag{7.2}$$

where $r = \ln\frac{S_T}{S_t}$. I have applied Equation (2.9), which implies that $\mathbb{E}[r] = 0$. $\sigma^2 = \mathbb{E}[r^2]$ is the standard deviation of the PDF of the log-return. One would use $\sigma^2_{realized}$ in the study of historical skewness or σ_i to study implied

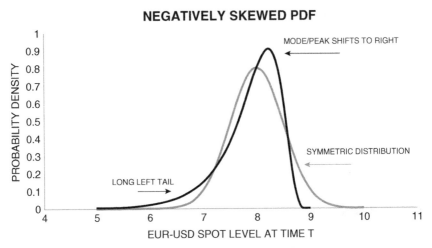

FIGURE 7.3 The figure shows a negatively skewed PDF (black) and a symmetric PDF (light gray). Note that the negatively skewed PDF has a long left tail. Down moves are therefore large. However, the peak of the negatively skewed distribution sits to the right of that of the symmetric distribution. This means that spot is more likely to move up than down.

skewness. A normal distribution has skew = 0. In Figure 7.3, skew < 0. One can show that skew is related to spot-vol correlation as follows:

$$\text{Skew} = \mathbb{E}\left[\frac{r^3}{\sigma^3}\right] = \frac{1}{\sigma^3}\mathbb{E}[r \times r^2],$$

$$= \frac{1}{\sigma^3}\text{Cov}[r, r^2],$$

$$= \text{Corr}[r, r^2] \times \frac{\text{Std Dev}[r^2]}{\sigma^2}. \qquad (7.3)$$

That is, skew is proportional to the correlation between the return r and the sqaured return r^2, which we know relates to volatility.

Equation (7.2) combined with the market prices of risk reversals and σ_i can be used to assess whether buying or selling risk reversals represents good economic value based on historic data in a way that is analogous to realized versus implied volatility that we discussed in Chapter 1. However, this is beyond the scope of this book and I refer interested readers to Neuberger (2012) and Kozhan, Neuberger, and Schneider (2013).

7.3   DELTA SPACE

Instead of specifying a strike K, FX options traders often specify the Δ_t of the option that they wish to trade, and a $\sigma_{implied}(\Delta_t)$. This practice is most common in the interbank market, although it is still used in the OTC market. Nevertheless, the idea remains important for FX options traders to understand.

Figure 7.4 shows the delta profile of a call option under low and high values of σ_i. When the option is OTM ($S_t < K$), then $\Delta_t < 50\%$. When the option is ATMS $S_t = K$, then $\Delta_t = 50\%$ approximately. Recall that Δ_t for a given option depends on σ_i because Δ_t is the probability of an ITM expiry. Market convention is to make all of these specifications using the BSM formula. I have therefore used the BSM model to generate Figure 7.4 and labeled delta as Δ_{BS} to make clear that it is calculated in this manner. Chapters 9 and 10 provide detailed formulae on this topic. Let us pursue the intuition here.

Suppose that the trader wishes to purchase an OTM EUR-USD call option and spot is trading at $S_t = 1.35$. She may ask her interbank broker for a price for a 25 delta call option. The buyer and seller agree a level of $\sigma_{implied} = 12\%$. This corresponds to the light gray line in Figure 7.4. Tracing this line, one can see that the 1.37 strike corresponds to a delta of 0.25. The traders would therefore trade the 1.37 strike and exchange $0.25 \times N$ EUR

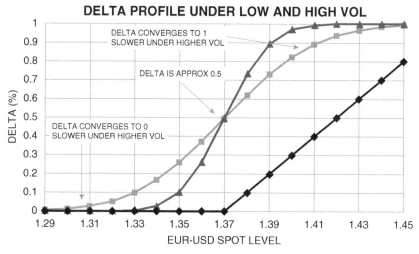

FIGURE 7.4   The figure shows $\Delta_{BS}(S, t, \sigma_{implied})$ for a $K = 1.37$ call option, calculated using $\sigma_{implied} = 4\%$ shown in dark gray and $\sigma_{implied} = 12\%$ shown in light gray.

between them so that they are both delta hedged. There are three important points to note here to build understanding of this concept.

First, the lower delta the strike, the further it is away from S_t. For example, had the trader asked for a 10 delta strike using $\sigma_{implied} = 12\%$, then applying the same logic as above, the strike would be 1.37 if $S_t = 1.33$. If spot were trading at $S_t = 1.37$, then one may expect the 10 delta strike to be roughly 1.41. The 25 delta strike was approximately 1.5% above S_t, whereas the 10 delta strike is approximately 3% above S_t.

Second, if $\sigma_{implied}$ were lower, say $\sigma_{implied} = 4\%$, corresponding to the dark gray line in Figure 7.4, then the same strike becomes lower delta. In the previous example with spot trading at $S_t = 1.35$, using $\sigma_{implied} = 4\%$, the 1.37 strike is 10 delta, not 25 delta. This makes sense because Δ_{BS} is close to the probability of an ITM expiry. If $\sigma_{implied}$ is lower and $S_t = 1.35$, then Prob($S_T > 1.37$) is lower.

Third, the process above is made precise via the BSM model. In practice, once the buyer and seller agree a $\sigma_{implied}$ at which they are both happy to trade, they will agree a K by inserting $\Delta_{BS} = 0.25$ (or whichever value they wish to trade) and $\sigma_{implied}$ into the BSM formula that relates Δ_{BS} and K (see Chapter 10).

7.4   SMILE IN DELTA SPACE

Figure 7.2 plotted the implied volatility smile in strike space (the x-axis displayed strike). This approach is commonly used in equity options trading. However, in FX, participants typically plot implied volatility in so-called *delta space*.

The idea behind delta space is that the x-axis is measured by Δ_{BS}. OTM calls appear on the right-hand side of the chart and OTM puts appear on the left-hand side. Figure 7.5 illustrates this.

One can convert between delta space and strike space via the BSM formula and I describe how to do this precisely in Chapter 10. At this stage the important points to understand are

- A lower delta strike corresponds to one that is further away from current spot. The strike of a 25 delta call or put is nearer to S_t than a 10 delta call or put.
- If volatility rises so that the line in Figure 7.5 moves upward in a parallel fashion, then the 25 delta call or put strike is further away because Prob($S_T > K$) rises with rising $\sigma_{implied}$. To maintain the same probability of an ITM expiry the strike must be further away.

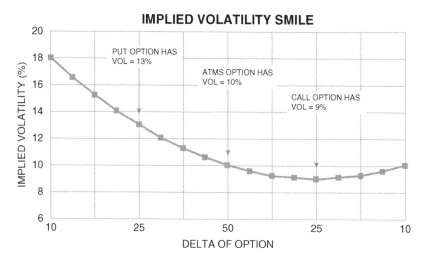

FIGURE 7.5 The figure shows an implied volatility smile $\sigma_{implied}(\Delta_{BS})$. In this example, the 25 delta call option trades at 9% and the 25 delta put option trades at 13%.

A final point to note is that the terminology that is used in practical trading relating to risk reversals is notoriously confusing. I provide a feature box to describe how risk reversals are bought and sold in practice.

TERMINOLOGY AROUND BUYING AND SELLING RISK REVERSALS

The terminology around trading risk reversals in FX markets can be confusing and prone to error. *Buying* a risk reversal does not necessarily mean that one is buying the call and selling the put, or that one is buying the put and selling the call! It means that the trader is buying whichever of the call and put trades at the higher value of $\sigma_{implied}(\Delta_{BS})$.

So for example, in AUD-JPY, AUD puts are typically priced at a higher $\sigma_{implied}(\Delta_{BS})$ than AUD calls. Therefore, *buying* AUD-JPY risk reversal means buying the put and selling the call. However, in EUR-NOK, for example, EUR calls are typically priced at a higher $\sigma_{implied}(\Delta_{BS})$ than EUR puts and therefore *buying* EUR-NOK risk reversal means buying EUR calls and selling puts.

(Continued)

The most common types of risk reversal traded are 25 delta and 10 delta. Suppose that the smile in Figure 7.5 corresponds to 1-month AUD-JPY. Then buying a 25 delta risk reversal corresponds to buying a 25 delta put at 13% and selling a 25 delta call at 9%.

More commonly, the trader would state that she bought the risk reversal at 4%. However, note that it is important to agree $\sigma_{implied}(\Delta_{BS})$ for one of the options with the counterparty. The reason is that this is a parameter that must be inserted into the BSM formula in order to agree the strike of the call and of the put. Failing to agree appropriate $\sigma_{implied}(\Delta_{BS})$ for the options can lead one counterparty to disadvantage. I describe this in detail under the heading *Smile Vega* in Section 7.5.

7.5   SMILE VEGA

Suppose that the trader trades a 25 delta risk reversal at 4%, where the put option trades at a higher $\sigma_{implied}(\Delta_{BS})$ than the call option. An issue that the counterparties may have in trading this structure is in setting the $\sigma_{implied}(\Delta_{BS})$ for each of the put and the call. These volatilities are known as volatility references. Consider the following example.

The buyer of the risk reversal (thereby buyer of the put) suggests a volatility reference for the put of 16% and therefore the call at 12%. The seller suggests, as in Figure 7.5, that the volatility references should be 13% and 9%.[2] On first inspection, this disagreement seems innocuous. After all, initially at least, a risk reversal structure has little vega because the trader has bought an option, but also sold an option that is struck a similar distance away. However, a more detailed examination reveals PnL implications for the buyer and seller.

If the seller were to agree implied volatilities of 16% and 12% for the put and call respectively, then the put and call would be further away from current spot than she had anticipated. The reason is that the strikes are set such that the approximate probability of an ITM expiry is 0.25 and such strikes are further from spot than if the traders were to agree lower implied volatilities. The seller realizes that if she wished to sell strikes that are further apart, then she should have charged more than 4% for the risk reversal. She

---

[2]This is an extreme example to illustrate the idea more clearly. In reality disagreements are typically of the order of 0.1% rather than 3%.

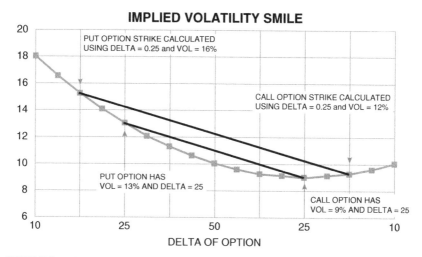

FIGURE 7.6 The lower black line shows the risk reversal that the seller had intended to trade at 4%. The higher black line shows the risk reversal that she will trade if she agrees to the higher vol references set by the buyer. Since the buyer's proposed volatility references are higher, the 25 delta strikes are further away from the spot level. From the point of view of the seller, these are lower delta strikes.
According to the seller, using the higher volatility references, the put should price at 15% and the call at 9.5%. The risk reversal should therefore trade at 5.5%. Selling at 4% is therefore a loss for her.

is at a disadvantage that grows the higher that the traders set volatility references. I illustrate this idea in Figure 7.6 and explain it further in its caption. The buyer of the risk reversal is said to be short smile vega, because the buyer benefits if implied volatilities are lower than the volatility references. The seller is said to be long smile vega.

There is no market standard mathematical definition for smile vega. I derive an equation that may serve the purpose in the next feature box.

CALCULATING SMILE VEGA

Let σ_h and σ_l denote the higher and lower references for the call respectively. In the example in the text these were 12% and 9%. If the seller agrees to use the buyer's reference of σ_h, then they will use this quantity

(Continued)

to calculate the strike that they trade. Denote the strike by K_h. Had they used σ_l, the strike would have been K_l, where clearly $K_h > K_l$.

The PnL implications of trading strike K_h rather than K_l can be calcuated as follows,

$$\text{PnL} = V_{BS}(K_h, \sigma_h) - V_{BS}\left(K_h, \sigma_l + \frac{\partial \sigma_{implied}(K_l)}{\partial K}(K_h - K_l)\right) \qquad (7.4)$$

$$= V_{BS}(K_h, \sigma_h) - V_{BS}(K_h, \sigma_l) - \frac{\partial V_{BS}(K_h, \sigma_l)}{\partial \sigma} \frac{\partial \sigma_{implied}(K_l)}{\partial K}(K_h - K_l)$$

$$= v_{BS}(K_h, \sigma_l)\left((\sigma_h - \sigma_l) - \frac{\partial \sigma_{implied}(K_l)}{\partial K}(K_h - K_l)\right), \qquad (7.5)$$

to first order. Equation (7.4) is the difference between the price at which the option has actually been traded and the model price calculated using the smile in Figure 7.6, which had lower volatility references. Taylor expanding and tidying up gives us Equation (7.5), which is intuitive. It says that the PnL to first order from trading an option using σ_h instead of σ_l is just the BSM vega times the difference in volatilities, plus an adjustment.

The adjustment is proportional to the local steepness in the smile around the strike being traded, and the difference between the strike traded and the strike that would have been traded at σ_l. Clearly, if $\sigma_{implied}(K)$ were constant as in the BSM model, then Equation (7.5) reduces to the BSM formula for vega.

Equation (7.5) makes clear that there are PnL implications from traders trading a risk reversal while disagreeing on vol references. The above equation is only zero if $\sigma_h = \sigma_l$. Note that this implies $K_h = K_l$.

7.5.1 Smile Vega Notionals

A standard risk reversal consists of equal notionals of the put and call. One way that traders use to circumvent disagreements over volatility references is to trade a contract known as a *risk reversal by smile vega*. The idea here is that, since the seller of the risk reversal believes in lower volatility references, if she agrees to trade at the higher volatility references, she can sell a higher notional of the put than she purchases of the call. By selling an option at a higher price, she is compensated for the PnL she loses on agreeing the higher volatility references.

Equation (7.5) provides the PnL of a single option that is traded using a different volatility reference. The risk reversal by smile vega has unequal notionals set such that the PnL across the trade is almost exactly zero according to this equation. Interbank market etiquette is for one counterparty to set the volatility reference, and the other side to decide whether one trades a standard risk reversal or a risk reversal by smile vega. This prevents an advantage to one counterparty.

7.6   SMILE DELTA

In FX markets, option traders typically calculate delta by asuming that the smile is fixed in delta space. That is, $\sigma_{implied}(\Delta_{BS})$ is constant until it is manually changed by the trader. FX options traders rarely inspect $\sigma_{implied}(K)$. This leads to a phenomenon known as smile delta. Consider the following example.

Suppose that the trader purchases a $\Delta_{BS}(S_t, t, \sigma_{implied}(25)) = 25\%$ OTM call option. If a short time δ later, S_t rises to $S_{t+\delta}$, then the call option becomes a higher delta call. Suppose that now $\Delta_{BS}(S_{t+\delta}, t, \sigma_{implied}(30))$. Figure 7.5 shows that $\sigma_{implied}(30) > \sigma_{implied}(25)$. Intuitively we see that, had the owner of the option executed $\Delta_{BS} = 25$ as her hedge, then she has benefited because the calculation of $\Delta_{BS}(S_t, t, \sigma_{implied}(25)) = 25\%$ did not account for the fact that $\sigma_{implied}(\Delta_{BS})$ for the option would also rise and raise the option value. The effect of an option moving to higher or lower points on the $\sigma_{implied}(\Delta_{BS})$ curve is often called *rolling* along the smile. In this case, the trader's option has rolled upward on the smile. Similarly, the trader would have lost had S_t fallen because her option would have rolled down on the smile.

In this scenario a trader would typically sell an additional quantity of spot beyond $\Delta_{BS}(S_t, t, \sigma_{implied}(25)) = 25\%$ to counter the effects of rolling on the smile. This additional quantity is known as smile delta. Again, there is no market standard formula for smile delta, but it can be calculated as described in the next feature box.

CALCULATING SMILE DELTA

Suppose that the trader purchases an option with $\Delta_{BS} = \alpha$ at a BSM implied volatility of $\sigma_{implied}(\alpha)$. S_t rises to $S_{t+\delta}$ and causing $\Delta_{BS} = \beta$. The change in value of the option is

$$V_{t+\delta} - V_t = V_{BS}(S_{t+\delta}, \sigma_{implied}(\beta)) - V_{BS}(S_t, \sigma_{implied}(\alpha))$$

$$= V_{BS}\left(S_{t+\delta}, \sigma_{implied}(\alpha) + \frac{\partial \sigma_{implied}(\alpha)}{\partial \Delta_{BS}}(\beta - \alpha)\right)$$

$$- V_{BS}(S_t, \sigma_{implied}(\alpha))$$

$$= V_{BS}(S_{t+\delta}, \sigma_{implied}(\alpha)) - V_{BS}(S_t, \sigma_{implied}(\alpha))$$

$$+ \frac{\partial V_{BS}(S_{t+\delta}, \sigma_{implied}(\alpha))}{\partial \sigma_{implied}} \frac{\partial \sigma_{implied}(\alpha)}{\partial \Delta_{BS}}(\beta - \alpha)$$

$$= \underbrace{\alpha(S_{t+\delta} - S_t)}_{\text{1. BSM Delta}} + \underbrace{v_{BS}(S_{t+\delta}, \sigma_{implied}(\alpha))\frac{\partial \sigma_{implied}(\alpha)}{\partial \Delta_{BS}}(\beta - \alpha)}_{\text{2. Smile Delta}}.$$

$$(7.6)$$

α in term 1 is the BSM delta. Term 2 represents smile delta. It depends on vega of the option and the steepness of the smile.

7.6.1 Considerations Relating to Smile Delta

Most modern risk management systems show traders their smile delta and it is therefore instinctive for traders to hedge smile delta. However, it is important for traders to think carefully about the assumptions that have gone into the calculation. The main assumption is that $\sigma_{implied}(\Delta_{BS})$ is constant until it is manually changed by the trader. This assumption leads us to a counterintuitive result.

Above, we said that when the smile is downward sloping (puts trade at a higher price than calls), then if the trader buys an option she should sell an additional amount of the underlying currency pair. The opposite true if the smile is upward sloping (calls trade higher than puts). However, earlier I discussed that a downward-sloping smile arises from negative spot-vol correlation. Therefore, if a trader purchases an option so that she is long volatility and spot rises, she loses PnL because implied volatility is expected to go down and then she loses more because she sold an additional amount of spot due to hedging her smile delta. One may argue that hedging smile delta added to the trader's risk rather than reducing it.

A better definition for smile delta could be argued to be

$$\text{Smile Delta} = \Delta(S_t, t, \sigma_i) - \Delta_{BS}(S_t, t, \sigma_{implied}(K)). \tag{7.7}$$

In words, it is the difference between the *true* delta of an option and that implied by the BSM model. The unsolved issue in options pricing is the form that $V(S_t, t, \sigma_i)$ and therefore $\Delta(S_t, t, \sigma)$ should take. However, in the absence of model panacea, traders must be careful to understand smile delta and beware that they may have to undo their smile delta hedges if they truly believe that spot-vol correlation will realize.

7.7   TRADER'S SUMMARY

- Vanna, skewness, and risk reversal are three closely related concepts.
- Vanna describes how an option portfolio's $v(S_t, t, \sigma_i)$ depends on S_t. It also describes how $\Delta(S_t, t, \sigma_i)$ depends on σ_i. It measures the portfolio's exposure to spot-vol correlation.
- Skewness describes the asymmetry in the spot PDF. Spot-vol correlation can lead to a skewed spot PDF.
- The term *risk reversal* has two meanings. First, it refers to the option structure of buying an OTM call and selling an OTM put, or vice versa. Second, it refers to the difference in $\sigma_{implied}$ between a call and put of the same delta. The most commonly traded are the 25 delta and 10 delta risk reversals.
- The buyer of the risk reversal is the buyer of the more expensive of the two options in terms of $\sigma_{implied}$. This could be the call or the put depending on the shape of the smile.
- FX options are modeled and often traded in delta space. The idea is that one sets a strike by setting a delta and a value of $\sigma_{implied}$. A given delta strike is further from spot the higher implied volatility.
- Delta space and risk reversal lead to smile vega. Smile vega means that volatility references matter, even on structures that have little vega.
- The smile is usually fixed in delta space. This leads to smile delta. However, smile delta can lead to counterintuitive trading; if spot-vol correlation is negative, a delta-hedging trader sells smile delta even though she is long vega and expects to profit if spot falls.

CHAPTER **8**

Volgamma, Butterfly, and Kurtosis

We began our study of smile in the previous chapter. This chapter extends our understanding of smile via study of three closely related ideas, namely volgamma, butterfly, and kurtosis.

Volgamma Volgamma describes how the $v(S_t, t, \sigma_i)$ of an option varies with σ_i. Its definition is

$$\text{Volgamma} \equiv \frac{\partial v(S_t, t, \sigma_i)}{\partial \sigma_i}. \tag{8.1}$$

Recall from Equation (5.3) that $v(S_t, t, \sigma_i)$ is independent of σ_i for an ATM option and hence its volgamma is zero. However, I show ahead that a long position in an OTM option is long volgamma.

From the previous definition we see that a trader with a long volgamma position, Volgamma > 0, derives longer $v(S_t, t, \sigma_i)$ when σ_i rises. If she wishes to return her $v(S_t, t, \sigma_i)$ to its previous level, then she can sell options. She may be glad to do so because she is selling after σ_i and therefore the price of options has risen. Similarly, she can buy options when σ_i falls.

This may sound familiar because it is analogous to trading long gamma. A trader with a long gamma position sells spot when it rises and buys spot when it falls. With a long volgamma position the trader sells volatility when σ_i rises and buys when σ_i falls. Similar to how a trader with a long gamma position benefits when there is high realized volatility, a trader with a long volgamma position benefits when there is high volatility of volatility itself.

Butterfly Analogous to risk reversal, the term *butterfly* has two meanings. First, it is an option structure that consists of selling an ATM straddle and buying a strangle. A strangle consists of an OTM call and an OTM put. I draw the payoff diagram of this structure in Figure 8.1.

Second, it is the cost of establishing this structure. To understand this, we must return to the idea from the previous chapter that $\sigma_{implied}$ depends on K or Δ. Loosely put, $\sigma_{implied}(\Delta)$ for the OTM call and OTM put is on average higher than for the ATM straddle. If the trader buys the butterfly, then she sells ATM options that have low $\sigma_{implied}(\Delta)$ and buys the options that have high $\sigma_{implied}(\Delta)$. In exchange for paying this *cost* she is long volgamma. I use the term *cost* loosely here because the buyer of the butterfly nevertheless receives premium. The cost she pays is relative to the BSM price. I explain this in more detail over the course of the chapter.

Kurtosis Like skewness, kurtosis is a feature of the PDF. In real markets, we observe more frequent extreme price movements than implied by the normal distribution. We also observe more days where price movements are contained relative to the normal distribution. The actual PDF that describes spot movements is *fat tailed* and *peaked* when compared with the normal (see Figure 8.3). This is called excess kurtosis.

Over the course of the chapter I described how volgamma, butterfly, and kurtosis are related to each other.

8.1   THE BUTTERFLY STRATEGY

A long butterfly strategy consists of purchasing an OTM call and an OTM put (this is known as a strangle) and selling a straddle as illustrated in Figure 8.1. A short butterfly strategy is the opposite: selling a strangle and buying a straddle. The structure is usually traded *vega neutral* at its inception, meaning that $v(S_t, t, \sigma_i) = 0$, even though $v \neq 0$ after S_t moves. More precisely, it is traded *Black-Scholes vega neutral* at inception, meaning that $v_{BS}(S_t, t, \sigma_{implied}) = 0$. Chapter 10 provides the functional form for v_{BS}. We will concern ourselves with the distinction between v and v_{BS} later in the chapter. For now, I proceeed by simply writing v and σ_i.

The vega neutrality of the structure occurs by construction in that the notional of the strangle is set such that $v(S_t, t, \sigma_i) = 0$. This means that the notional of the strangle is larger than that of the straddle. The reason is that ATM options have more vega than OTM options for a given notional (recall this from Section 5.5). I explain this in more detail in the caption in Figure 8.1. The figure also illustrates, literally, the reason that the strategy is called a butterfly!

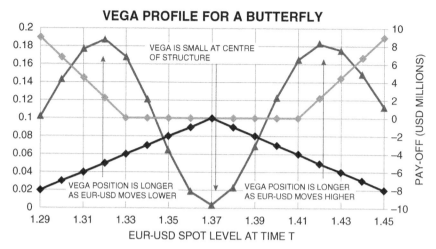

FIGURE 8.1   The figure shows the vega profile of a vega neutral butterfly (dark gray line, left axis). It also shows the payoff structure of the four individual options that make up the butterfly. A butterfly consists of short a straddle (black, right axis) and long a strangle (light gray, right axis). For the structure to be vega neutral at spot 1.37, the notionals of the straddle strikes must be larger than those of the straddle strike. In this structure, I show the vega profile of a 1-month butterfly with $\sigma_{implied} = 8\%$. The notional of the strangle strikes is 2.25 that of the straddle. This is the reason that the light gray lines are more steeply sloped than the black lines.

The buyer of the butterfly receives premium. The reason is that the straddle is more expensive than the strangle, even though the strangle is larger in notional. Inspecting the butterfly payoff shows us that the trader would buy the butterfly if she believes that spot will remain unchanged (she is short the straddle and receives premium) and she believes that if spot moves, then it moves a significant distance away from the straddle (she is long a strangle in larger notional so her payoff becomes positive again for large moves).

8.2   VOLGAMMA AND BUTTERFLY

Figure 8.1 shows that the trader's vega starts flat, $v(S_t, t, \sigma_i) = 0$, but becomes long if S_t moves in either direction. I return to the dependence of $v(S_t, t, \sigma_i)$ on S_t later. Here, I focus on how the structure behaves if σ_i changes, rather than if S_t changes.

First, suppose that σ_i rises. To understand how the vega profile changes, recall from Figures 5.2 and 5.4 in Chapter 5 that for a single option of

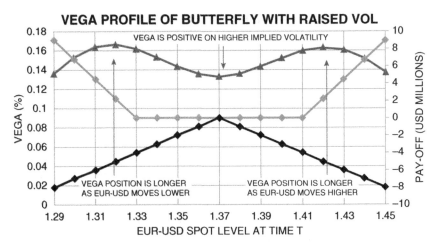

FIGURE 8.2 The figure shows the vega profile of the same butterfly structure as in Figure 8.1. However, I use $\sigma_{implied} = 12\%$. The vega (dark gray line) is now positive at $S_t = 1.37$ and it is also flatter across values of S.

strike K, raising σ_i does not change $v(S, t, \sigma_i)$ if $S = K$, but for $S \neq K$ $v(S, t, \sigma_i)$ rises. In the case of the butterfly, therefore, $S_t \approx K$ for the straddle and so its contribution to the overall vega of the structure remains unchanged. However, the strangle gains vega. This means that the overall structure becomes longer vega at S_t. That is, $v(S_t, t, \sigma_2) > v(S_t, t, \sigma_1)$ for $\sigma_2 > \sigma_1$. Figure 8.2 shows the vega profile of the same butterfly structure as that in Figure 8.1, but having raised σ_i.

Since σ_i moving higher has left the trader longer $v(S_t, t, \phi)$ she may sell options to return her vega position back to zero. I leave it to the reader to work through similar logic to see that the trader would have been left shorter $v(S_t, t, \phi)$ had σ_i moved lower. It is clear that the butterfly structure is long volgamma.

8.3 KURTOSIS

Figure 8.3 shows two PDFs for spot. The black line shows a normal distribution. The light gray line is a so-called *leptokurtic* distribution, meaning that it exhibits excess kurtosis compared with the normal.

Consider a situation in which traders have priced the black distribution into options. However, market participants begin to realize that the actual

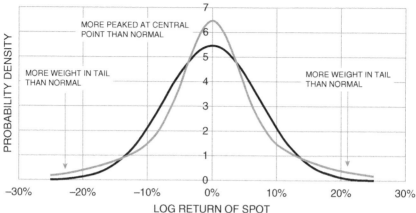

FIGURE 8.3 The black line shows a normal distribution with $\sigma_i = 8\%$. The light gray line shows a leptokurtic distribution that also has $\sigma_i = 8\%$. Note that the leptokurtic distribution has a higher peak than the normal. It is therefore more likely that spot will remain unchanged than implied by the normal. The leptokurtic distribution also has more weight in the tails than the normal. It is therefore more likely that spot exhibits extreme moves than implied by the normal.

distribution is more like the light gray line. First, they realize that the peak means that spot is more likely to remain in the center of the distribution than is currently priced. This means that they sell ATM straddles to profit from the additional probability that we observe only very small moves. Second, they realize that spot is also more likely to exhibit a very large positive or negative return than is priced. They therefore look to purchase OTM strangles. That is, market particpants buy the butterfly.

This example makes clear that the more kurtosis there is in the spot PDF, the higher the fair price should be for the butterfly. In the next section, I discuss how this pricing feeds into the volatility smile.

8.4 SMILE

In Figure 7.5 I argued that the downward slope existed due to negative spot-vol correlation. I did not comment on the convexity of the smile. For simplicity and to separate the two effects, let us consider the case where spot-vol correlation is zero. In that case one may expect a symmetric smile, such as that drawn in Figure 8.4.

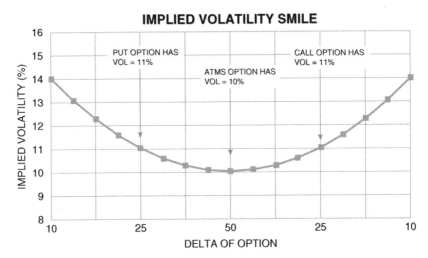

FIGURE 8.4 The figure shows $\sigma_{implied}(\Delta_{BS})$ assuming that the PDF of spot returns is leptokurtic and that there is no spot-vol correlation or, equivalently, no risk reversal. The smile is therefore symmetric.

The BSM model suggests that $\sigma_{implied}(\Delta)$ is constant and that this corresponds to a log-normal spot PDF. In the previous section, we showed that excess kurtosis leads to traders wanting to sell ATM options and buy OTM strangles. The method through which this gets reflected in market prices is through increasing convexity in the smile.

Figure 8.4 shows that the 25 delta put and 25 delta call are priced at 11%, whereas the ATMS option is priced at 10%. Further increasing the amount of kurtosis in the PDF would increase the price of the call and put relative to the ATMS option.

8.5   BUTTERFLIES AND SMILE VEGA

Market practice in trading a butterfly can be understood as follows. The most commonly traded butterflies are 25 delta and 10 delta. Suppose that a buyer and seller agree to trade the 25 delta butterfly at 0.5%. The buyer of the butterfly sells ATM straddles and purchases a strangle. Just like with risk reversal, they must agree a volatility reference. Suppose that they agree that the reference for the ATM is 10%. The next step is setting the strikes of the strangles.

The strikes of the strangles are set by inserting 10.5% and $\Delta_{BS} = 0.25$ into the BSM formula for the call and calculating K. The same is done for the put. There are at least three important points to note here.

First, the smile shown in Figure 8.4 is symmetric and so the call and put are priced at the same $\sigma_{implied}$. However, in general there is a risk reversal and so smiles look more like Figure 7.2. Nevertheless, the market butterfly always involves inserting identical $\sigma_{implied}$ into the call and put to calculate the strikes.

It is more complicated for a trader to use her marked smile to calculate the price for the butterfly than for the risk reversal. In the case of the risk reversal, she simply took her $\sigma_{implied}(\Delta_{BS} = 0.25)$ mark for each of the call and the put and subtracted one from the other. However, in the case of the butterfly she is forced to insert the same $\sigma_{implied}$ into the call and the put, even though they are marked at different levels.

The approach that many options systems take is an iterative one. The basic idea is to calculate a starting value using the smile as

$$\text{Starting Value} = \frac{1}{2} \left(\sigma_{implied}(\Delta_{BS}^{\text{call}} = 0.25) + \sigma_{implied}(\Delta_{BS}^{\text{put}} = 0.25) \right).$$

Next, insert this value into the BSM formula for $\sigma_{implied}$ for both the call and the put. Adjust the value higher or lower until the PnL of trading the call and the put is zero. Finally, subtract $\sigma_{implied}(\text{ATM})$ to get the butterfly.

Second, just like with risk reversal, smile vega is important. Again, suppose that the traders agree to trade the butterfly at 0.5%. If the buyer sets the volatility reference for the ATM strike at 11%, then the strangle strikes will be calculated using $\sigma_{implied} = 11.5\%$. Clearly, these strikes will be further away from S_t than had the ATM been set at 10% and therefore the strangle strikes at 10.5%. The convex shape in Figure 8.4 shows that strikes that are further from S_t should trade at higher levels of $\sigma_{implied}$ than strikes that are nearer S_t. The buyer will therefore gain because she is able to purchase strikes that are further away at the same price.

8.6 TRADER'S SUMMARY

- Volgamma, kurtosis, and butterfly are three closely related concepts.
- Volgamma describes how an option portfolio's $v(S_t, t, \sigma_i)$ depends on σ_i. It measures the portfolio's exposure to volatility of volatility.

- Kurtosis describes the weight in the center and the tails of the spot PDF. Movements in σ_i can lead to a leptokurtic spot PDF.
- The term *butterfly* has two meanings. First, it refers to the option structure of buying a strangle and selling an ATM straddle, or vice versa. Second, it refers to the difference in $\sigma_{implied}$ of the strangle and the straddle. The strangle is priced by inserting the same value of $\sigma_{implied}$ into the BSM formua for both the OTM call and the OTM put.
- The most commonly traded butterflies are the 25 delta and 10 delta.
- The buyer of the butterfly is the counterparty buying the strangle, or wing options.
- The butterfly is usually calculated using an iterative scheme.
- The buyer of the butterfly is short smile vega.

CHAPTER 9

Black-Scholes-Merton Model

The objective in this chapter is to develop a deep and, most importantly, intuitive, understanding of the seminal contributions to option pricing made by Black and Scholes (1973) and Merton (1973). In essence, the BSM approach made mathematical modeling assumptions that allowed the authors to derive a functional form for the option valuation function, namely $V_{BS}(S_t, t, \sigma_{implied})$.[1]

Even though it has long been established that real markets deviate substantially from BSM formula, their model still provides the building blocks for the pricing of FX options and valuable insight into how to trade them. For example, we have seen in previous chapters that traders use $\sigma_{implied}$ in many contexts. Despite the presence of smile directly contradicting the BSM model, traders prefer to perturb the BSM model by making $\sigma_{implied}$ a function of K, than to discard it.

I split the study of BSM into two parts. This chapter studies the derivation of $V_{BS}(S_t, t, \sigma_{implied})$ and provides its functional form. Until now, we have assumed that interest rates are zero. This chapter introduces interest rates into our analysis.

In Chapter 10 I discuss the many equations that follow from V_{BS}. I provide the functional forms of the Greeks delta, gamma, theta, vanna, and volgamma. I also provide some overdue definitions such as that of the ATM strike.

---

[1]Garman and Kohlhagen (1983) modified the Black-Scholes approach in a manner appropriate for FX markets by accounting for the fact that both the foreign and domestic underlying currencies pay interest and this is the path that I follow in this chapter.

9.1 THE LOG-NORMAL DIFFUSION MODEL

The BSM model makes the mathematical assumption that S_t follows

$$\frac{dS_t}{S_t} = \mu dt + \sigma dZ_t, \tag{9.1}$$

where μ is the so-called *drift* term, and Z_t is a Brownian motion. Perhaps the easiest way to understand this equation is through discretizing it. To do the discretization accurately, we have to apply Ito's Lemma to Equation (9.1). Readers unfamiliar with Ito's Lemma may refer to, in order of increasing detail, Hull (2011), Shreve (2000), or Duffie (2001). However, I urge even readers unfamiliar with Ito's Lemma and who do not wish to consult a separate text to plough on. The main challenge here is conceptual, not technical.

The discretized version of the previous equation is

$$\ln \frac{S_{t+\delta}}{S_t} = (\mu - \frac{1}{2}\sigma^2)\delta + \sigma(Z_{t+\delta} - Z_t), \tag{9.2}$$

where δ is a period of time. $Z_{t+\delta} - Z_t$ is a normally distributed random variable with variance δ. σ is the volatility.

First, set $\delta = 1$ year. Note that σ is of the order of 10% in FX markets. Therefore, σ^2 is typically small ($\tilde{0}.01$). I therefore ignore σ^2 for now. Equation (9.2) then says that the annual return of spot is μ plus some randomness. If $\sigma = 0$, then the log return would be μ. In reality, $\sigma > 0$ and so only the expected return is μ.

BSM originally wrote this equation with the intention of valuing equity options. The post–World War II average annualized return of the S&P 500 index is approximately 8%. For the S&P equity index at least, one can imagine $\mu = 8\%$ to be the right order of magnitude. However, μ is a quantity that is notoriously difficult to estimate. Fortunately, we shall see that one does not need to know μ to price options. Indeed, this was one of the main insights stemming from the BSM approach.

9.2 THE BSM PARTIAL DIFFERENTIAL EQUATION (PDE)

BSM assumes that σ is fixed. The value of an option is therefore given by $V_t = V(S_t, t)$ and σ is a parameter. I continue from Equation 2.7 in Section 2.6.

Recall that we had considered a portfolio consisting of an option and short an amount Δ_t of the underlying currency.

First, I rewrite Equation 2.7 in differential form. I also apply Ito's Lemma to add in the *further terms* that I had left out earlier:

$$dW_t = \underbrace{\frac{\partial V(S_t, t)}{\partial t} dt}_{\text{1. Exposure to Time}} + \underbrace{\left(\frac{\partial V(S_t, t)}{\partial S} - \Delta_t \right) dS_t}_{\text{2. Exposure to Spot Moving}} + \underbrace{\frac{\partial^2 V(S_t, t)}{\partial S^2} dS_t^2}_{\text{3. Gamma Term}}. \quad (9.3)$$

Recall also from Chapter 2 that a delta-hedging trader holds $\Delta_t = \frac{\partial V(S_t, t)}{\partial S}$. At this stage, we do not know the functional form of $V(S_t, t)$, but we will shortly, and therefore the assumption that the trader is able to hold $\frac{\partial V(S_t, t)}{\partial S}$ of the underlying will be justified. This assumption means that term 2 disappears. μ would have entered through the term dS_t but it has been eliminated with term 2.

Finally, note that $dS_t^2 = \sigma^2 S_t^2 dt$. I provide some intuition behind this result in the feature box.

BROWNIAN MOTION

A Brownian motion Z_t has the property that $Z_{t+\delta} - Z_t \sim \mathcal{N}(0, \delta)$. That is, its variance grows linearly with time. Think of dZ_t as $Z_{t+\delta} - Z_t$ for arbitrarily small δ, $\delta = dt$. Clearly,

$$\mathbb{E}_t[dZ_t] = 0,$$

$$\mathbb{E}_t[dZ_t^2] = dt. \quad (9.4)$$

The second line is simply the variance of dZ_t. Our next task is to show that $dZ_t^2 = dt$, even without the expectation. First, note that $(Z_{t+\delta} - Z_t)^2$ is a chi-squared distributed random variable,

$$\frac{(Z_{t+\delta} - Z_t)^2}{\delta} \sim \chi_1^2. \quad (9.5)$$

(Continued)

Applying standard results relating to chi-squared random variables,

$$\mathbb{E}_t[(Z_{t+\delta} - Z_t)^2] = \delta,$$

$$Var[(Z_{t+\delta} - Z_t)^2] = \delta^2 Var(\chi_1^2) = 2\delta^2. \qquad (9.6)$$

As we make δ arbitrarily small, $\delta \to dt$, Equation (9.6) vanishes as it is of order dt^2. So, indeed, we have $dZ_t^2 = dt$.

Applying this result to Equation (9.1) gives us the required result that

$$dS_t^2 = \mu^2 S_t^2 dt^2 + \sigma^2 S_t^2 dt + \mu\sigma S_t^2 dt^{\frac{3}{2}}$$

$$= \sigma^2 S_t^2 dt \qquad (9.7)$$

because the other terms are of a smaller order of magnitude than dt.

Equation (9.3) therefore becomes

$$dW_t = \left(\frac{\partial V(S_t, t)}{\partial t} + \frac{\partial^2 V(S_t, t)}{\partial S^2} \sigma^2 S_t^2 \right) dt. \qquad (9.8)$$

The important point to note here is that there is no longer any uncertainty. All of the uncertainty in the BSM model came from the Brownian motion dZ_t term, but through delta hedging, the trader has removed it.

One may argue that this uncertainty has only been removed for an instant of time. The idea in the BSM model, however, is that the trader rebalances her deltas continuously in time. That is, an instant of time dt later, she adjusts her Δ_{t+dt} so that she has removed the uncertainty once more. She gamma trades in continuous time. In real markets, traders rebalance at discrete instants of time, rather than continuously. Therefore, there remains some uncertainty and this leads to PnL variance. Nevertheless, at this stage, let us continue to understand the BSM argument by assuming that continual and costless rebalancing is possible.

Suppose that interest rates are zero. This implies that $dW_t = 0$. This can be understood as follows. First, suppose that $dW_t > 0$. If this were true, then one could simply borrow without cost to finance the portfolio W_t, and make an arbitrage profit[2] over the time period dt. Similarly, if $dW_t < 0$, then

---

[2]An arbitrage refers to a risk-free profit. In the BSM approach, the presence of professional arbitragers in the market rules out arbitrage opportunities from existing.

one could make an arbitrage profit over the time period dt by shorting the portfolio W_t.

In the case of zero interest rates, Equation (9.8) can be written as

$$\frac{\partial V(S_t, t)}{\partial t} = -\frac{\partial^2 V(S_t, t)}{\partial S^2} \sigma^2 S_t^2.$$

Substituting Equations (3.1) and (4.2) we have

$$\frac{\theta(S_t, t)}{S_t} = 100 \Gamma_{trader}(S_t, t)\sigma^2. \tag{9.9}$$

This is the famous BSM partial differential equation (PDE) written in perhaps its simplest form. Again, let us take EUR-USD as our example. The left-hand side is the theta measured over an instant of time, in EUR. The right-hand side is the trader's gamma measured in EUR multiplied by volatility σ. The equation tells us that gamma and theta can be mapped from one to the other, simply by multiplying by σ^2.

More generally, interest rates are not zero. Let r_f represent the continuously compounded interest rate in the base currency, namely EUR in the example of EUR-USD, and let r_d represent the continuously compounded interest rate in the numeraire currency, namely USD in the example of EUR-USD. Suppose also that the trader does not face borrowing or lending transaction costs or constraints.

Assume that the trader starts without any investment capital. She must finance her entire position. In order to finance the portfolio $W_t = V(S_t, t) - \Delta_t S_t$, she must borrow an amount W_t. The cost of this is $r_d W_t dt$ over the next increment of time. She must also borrow $\Delta_t = \frac{\partial V(S_t, t)}{\partial S}$ of the base currency (e.g. EUR) in order to short sell it if she is hedging a call option position. Her cost is $r_f \Delta_t S_t$. For there to be no arbitrage, after the time period dt the trader must still have zero capital, because there is no risk. Therefore the following equation must hold true:

$$\underbrace{\frac{\partial V(S_t, t)}{\partial t} + \frac{\partial^2 V(S_t, t)}{\partial S^2} \sigma^2 S_t^2}_{\text{1. Performance of portfolio } W_t.} - \underbrace{r_d \left(V(S_t, t,) - S_t \frac{\partial V(S_t, t)}{\partial S} \right)}_{\text{2. Financing portfolio } W_t.}$$

$$- \underbrace{r_f S_t \frac{\partial V(S_t, t)}{\partial S}}_{\text{3. Financing base currency.}} = 0.$$

Rearranging and tidying up gives us the full BSM PDE:

$$\frac{\partial V(S_t, t)}{\partial t} + \frac{\partial^2 V(S_t, t)}{\partial S^2}\sigma^2 S_t^2 - r_d V(S_t, t,) + (r_d - r_f)\frac{\partial V(S_t, t)}{\partial S} = 0. \quad (9.10)$$

In the case of a call option, the boundary condition is $V(S_T, T) = \max(S_T - K, 0)$ and it is $V(S_T, T) = \max(K - S_T, 0)$ for a put option.

Earlier, I discussed borrowing EUR to short sell. This is true in the case of a call option. In the case of a put option, one would borrow USD and short sell. However, Equation (9.10) looks the same.

There are several methods that one can use to solve this PDE in order to calculate explicitly $V(S_t, t)$ (see Shreve, 2000). The solution turns out to be

$$V_{BS}(S_t, t, \sigma_{implied}) = \lambda[S_t e^{-r_f \tau} N(\lambda d_1) - K e^{-r_d \tau} N(\lambda d_2)], \quad (9.11)$$

$$d_1 = \frac{\ln(S_t/K) + (r_d - r_f + \sigma^2_{implied}/2)T}{\sigma_{implied}T},$$

$$d_2 = d_1 - \sigma_{implied}T.$$

$N(x)$ is the standard normal CDF. $\lambda = 1$ for a call option and -1 for a put option. Now that we have the solution, I have labeled V as V_{BS} and σ as $\sigma_{implied}$.

Next, I show the reader how to relate this PDE back to our studies in the early chapters of this text. This is the topic of the next section.

9.3 FEYNMAN-KAC

Feynman and Kac showed that the PDE in Equation (9.10) is equivalent to calculating the following expectation for a call option,

$$V(S_t, t) = e^{-r_d \tau}\mathbb{E}_t[\max(S_T - K, 0)], \quad (9.12)$$

where

$$\frac{dS_t}{S_t} = (r_d - r_f)dt + \sigma dZ_t. \quad (9.13)$$

I do not re-derive the Feynman-Kac solution here and I refer interested readers to Duffie (2001) for a rigorous analysis. However, the equivalence between (9.12) and (9.10) is intuitive. Equation (9.12) clearly satisifes the boundary condition $V(S_T, T) = \max(S_T - K, 0)$. As long as the left-hand side is a function of S_t and t only, then we can apply the logic of the previous section and Ito's Lemma to show that $V(S_t, t)$ satisfies Equation (9.10).

It is important to understand the main implications of Equation (9.12). First, note that it is almost identical to Equation (2.2) but for two main differences.

First, the previous equation contains r_d explicitly and r_f implicitly via S_T. In Chapter 2 we set interest rates to zero and therefore these parameters do not appear in Equation (2.2).

The second difference is more subtle, but also more important. It relates to the probability measure under which the expectation is taken. This is the topic of the next section.

9.4   RISK-NEUTRAL PROBABILITIES

Consider the case of zero interest rates again. In Equation (2.2) the reader was led to believe that the expectation was taken under an objective probability measure. By this I mean that the trader uses Equation (9.1) and a value for μ based on a forecast or empirical work to calculate $\mathbb{E}[\max(S_T - K, 0)]$ and value the option. For example, in the case of an option on the S&P 500 index, one may be tempted to use $\mu = 8\%$ based on historic data. Such an approach would lead traders to value ATMS call options higher than ATMS put options, because spot is expected to rise at 8% per year.

However, note that the BSM valuation equation, Equation (9.12), does not even contain μ. Recall that we removed it by setting $\Delta_t = \frac{\partial V_{BS}(S_t, t)}{\partial S}$. Therefore, even though the trader expects that S_t will appreciate at 8% per year, she values the ATMS call at the same price as the ATMS put.

One can understand this as follows. Suppose that a market participant purchases a 1-year call option with the objective expectation that S_t will rise by 8% over the next year. The option trader sells the call option and then delta hedges by purchasing the underlying spot. By purchasing the exact amount of spot as her hedge that the option is exposed to, namely Δ_t, she is able to make back what she loses on the option position. Hence, for the seller μ does not matter.

Perhaps a clearer way of seeing this is via put–call parity. Again, assume zero interest rates. The trader sells the ATMS call and buys the ATMS put. Since the BSM model prices the ATMS call and put at the same price, her cost for setting up this portfolio is zero. Simultaneously, the trader purchases spot in notional equal to the options. Clearly, her PnL is zero everywhere, even if spot appreciates at a rate of 8% per year.

The key point to note is that delta hedging removes any exposure to spot. Exposure to interest rates remains because implementing delta hedging involves borrowing and lending. Delta-hedged options therefore expose the traders to volatility only.

9.5 PROBABILITY OF EXCEEDING THE BREAKEVEN IN THE BSM MODEL

Recall that in Section 6.5 I calculated that the probability that spot exceeds the breakeven of an ATMS straddle was 42% in the context of the normal model. The feature box shows that the same result is approximately true in the context of the BSM model.

PROBABILITY OF EXCEEDING THE BREAKEVEN

First, discretize Equation (9.13):

$$\ln\frac{S_{t+\delta}}{S_t} = (r_d - r_f - \frac{1}{2}\sigma^2)\delta + \sigma(Z_{t+\delta} - Z_t).$$

Again I assume zero interest rates. Also, note again that since σ is of the order of 10% in FX markets, σ^2 is small. I therefore ignore the σ^2 term. The probability of exceeding the breakeven is then calculated as follows:

$$2 \times \text{Prob}_t\left(\ln\frac{S_T}{S_t} > \frac{4.2\sigma\sqrt{n}}{100}\right) = 2 \times \text{Prob}_t\left(\sigma(Z_T - Z_t) > \frac{4.2\sigma\sqrt{n}}{100}\right)$$

$$= 2 \times \text{Prob}_t\left(\epsilon\frac{\sqrt{n}}{\sqrt{365}} > \frac{4.2\sqrt{n}}{100}\right)$$

$$= 2 \times \left(1 - N\left(\frac{4.2\sqrt{365}}{100}\right)\right)$$

$$= 42\%.$$

Again, the factor of 2 comes from the fact that the breakeven can be exceeded from above or below.

9.6   TRADER'S SUMMARY

- BSM is a log-normal diffusion model.
- The key idea is to construct a risk-free portfolio by delta hedging continuously in time. This leads to the famous BSM PDE.
- The BSM PDE shows that gamma and theta can be mapped to each other via the volatility.
- The Feynman-Kac theorem shows us that the price of an option is the expectation of its payoff, as discussed in Chapter 2. However, importantly, this expectation is taken under a risk-neutral rather than objective probability measure.

CHAPTER 10

The Black-Scholes Greeks

This chapter discusses the many equations that follow from V_{BS}. I provide the BSM functional forms of the Greeks delta, forward delta, gamma, theta, vanna, and volgamma. I also introduce the concept of dual delta and use it to show how an option exposes the trader to the well-known *carry trade*.

10.1 SPOT DELTA, DUAL DELTA, AND FORWARD DELTA

10.1.1 Spot Delta

The Black-Scholes delta is calculated by differentiating Equation (9.12). I state the result before breaking it down into its components:

$$\Delta_{BS} \equiv \frac{\partial V_{BS}}{\partial S} = \lambda e^{-r_f \tau} N(\lambda d_1) \quad \text{where} \tag{10.1}$$

$$d_1 = \frac{\ln \frac{f_t}{K} + \frac{1}{2}\sigma^2_{implied}\tau}{\sigma\sqrt{\tau}} \text{and } f_t = S_t e^{(r_d - r_d)\tau}.$$

$\lambda = 1$ for a call option and $\lambda = -1$ for a put option. The intuition explaining the behavior of delta was captured by the simple model in (2.8) that showed that delta is the probability of an ITM expiry. This idea remains approximately true in the log-normal BSM model. The feature box shows that the risk-neutral probability of an ITM expiry in the BSM model is $N(d_2)$. Figure 10.1 plots $\Delta_{BS} - N(d_2)$ for a reasonable range of real G10 FX market parameters showing that the difference is usually small, but grows with τ and $\sigma_{implied}$. However, even in the context of the BSM model, thinking of delta as the probability of an ITM expiry remains a good approximation in normal FX market conditions.

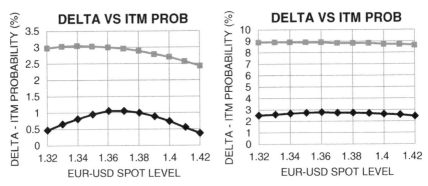

FIGURE 10.1 The figures show the difference between the BSM delta of a 1.37 EUR-USD call option and the risk-neutral probability of an ITM expiry. The left chart uses $\sigma_{implied} = 10\%$. The black line corresponds to a 1-month option and the light gray line to a 1-year option. At these typical levels of market parameters, the difference is small. For a 1-month option, the maximum difference is around 1% and for a 1-year option it is around 3%. The right chart shows more extreme market parameters. In 2008, during the financial crisis, EUR-USD volatility reached over 25%. I therefore conduct the same analysis for a 1-month option (black) and 1-year option (light gray). The maximum differences are now around 3% and 9 % respectively.

RISK-NEUTRAL PROBABILITY OF AN ITM EXPIRY IN THE BSM MODEL

The discretized version of Equation (9.13) is

$$\ln \frac{S_T}{S_t} = (r_d - r_f - \frac{1}{2}\sigma^2)\tau + \sigma(Z_T - Z_t). \tag{10.2}$$

Therefore,

$$\text{Prob}_t(S_T > K) = \text{Prob}_t(\ln S_T > \ln K)$$

$$= \text{Prob}_t(\ln S_t + (r_d - r_f - \frac{1}{2}\sigma^2)\tau + \sigma\sqrt{\tau}\epsilon > \ln K)$$

$$= \text{Prob}_t\left(\epsilon \leq \frac{\ln \frac{S_t}{K} + (r_d - r_f - \frac{1}{2}\sigma^2\tau)}{\sigma\sqrt{\tau}}\right)$$

$$= N(d_2), \tag{10.3}$$

where $d_2 = \frac{\ln \frac{S_t}{K} - \frac{1}{2}\sigma^2_{implied}\tau}{\sigma\sqrt{\tau}}$ and I set $\sigma = \sigma_{implied}$.

Interest Rates Interest rates enter (10.1) in two places. First, d_1 depends on the f_t and hence on the difference between domestic and foreign interest rates, $r_d - r_f$. The absolute levels of r_d and r_f do not affect d_1. The reason for this dependence can be understood as follows. f_t can be thought of as the expected future value of the spot exchange rate. To see this, continue from Equation (10.2) and calculate $\mathbb{E}_t[S_T]$,

$$\mathbb{E}_t[S_T] = \mathbb{E}_t[S_t e^{(r_d-r_f-\frac{1}{2}\sigma^2)\tau+\sigma(Z_T-Z_t)}]$$
$$= f_t. \tag{10.4}$$

If f_t is large, then it is more likely that the option will expire ITM and that the holder of the option will exercise. It therefore makes sense for the seller of the option to hold more of the base currency as a hedge and hence Δ_{BS} increases with increasing f_t.

Second, Δ_{BS} depends explicitly on r_f through the term $e^{-r_f\tau}$. The intuition behind this dependence is as follows. If a call option expires in the money, then the seller of the option must deliver the base currency to the buyer of the option in the notional amount. If the option seller were to dynamically hedge her position, then she would hold a long position in the base currency as a hedge. However, while holding the base currency, she earns interest that is paid in the base currency. The $e^{-r_f\tau}$ term acts to ensure that she does not accumulate more of the base currency than the notional of the option.

Finally, as an aside, note that if investors are risk neutral and if interest rates are zero, then Equation (10.4) reduces to Equation (2.9).

10.1.2 The ATM Strike and the Delta-Neutral Straddle

I introduced the ATM strike in Chapter 1, but did not discuss its origins. With the formula for Δ_{BS} in place it is straightforward to derive the ATM strike.

ATM is defined as the strike at which the delta of the call option plus the delta of the put option is zero according to the BSM formula. Therefore, we require

$$e^{-r_f\tau}N(d_1) - e^{-r_f\tau}N(-d_1) = 0.$$

Setting $d_1 = 0$ solves the above equation. Therefore, $K = S_t e^{\frac{1}{2}\sigma^2\tau}$.

The delta-neutral straddle (DNS) consists of purchasing a call and a put of the same strike such that the BSM delta of the structure is zero. The DNS is therefore struck at the ATM point.

Note that a DNS will have a smile delta component. It therefore only has zero BSM delta, and not necessarily zero delta.

10.1.3 Dual Delta

The dual delta, which I denote by Δ_K, is the sensitivity of the option price to a change in its strike. Again, let us begin by stating the Black-Scholes calculation for Δ_K, before interpreting this quantity:

$$\Delta_K \equiv \frac{\partial C}{\partial K} = -\lambda e^{-r_d \tau} N(\lambda d_2) \quad \text{where} \quad d_2 = \frac{\ln \frac{f_t}{K} - \frac{1}{2}\sigma_{implied}^2 \tau}{\sigma_{implied}\sqrt{\tau}}. \quad (10.5)$$

Δ_K has two useful interpretations. The first is that it is the price in of a digital option with payout of one unit, struck at K. This is because a digital option can be replicated using an infinitesimally small call spread, scaled so that the payout is equal to 1, as discussed in Section 2.8.

Another interpretation of Δ_K is that it is the delta of the option from the point of view of the investor based in the base currency. To make this clear, let us take the example of a EUR-call USD-put option contract sold by an American bank that bases its accounting in USD to a European, EUR-based bank.

1. The European bank agrees to buy the EUR-call USD-put option contract from the American bank, paying the option premium in USD.
2. The American bank buys Δ_S EUR as a hedge. Correspondingly, the European bank must sell Δ_S EUR as a hedge. It does so at the spot rate S_t and therefore receives $\Delta_S S_t$ USD.
3. The European bank pays the option premium of $V_{BS}(S_t, K)$ to the American bank. The European bank is left with a USD amount of $\Delta_S S_t - V_{BS}(S_t, K) = e^{-r_{eur}\tau} N(d_1)S_t - e^{-r_{usd}\tau}[fN(d_1) - KN(d_2)]$, where I have used Equation (9.12) for $V_{BS}(S_t, K)$. Substituting in our equation for f_t from Equation (10.2) we see that the European bank is left holding a long position of $KN(d_2)e^{-r_{usd}\tau}$ USD. The notional of the option in USD is simply K and so, per unit of notional, the European bank holds $N(d_2)e^{-r_{usd}\tau}$, which is precisely minus the dual delta that was given in Equation (10.5).

In summary, the above example shows that, if option premiums are paid in USD, Δ_K is simply the delta from the point of view of an option holder thinking of the option as a put option on USD-EUR as opposed to a call on EUR-USD.

10.1.4 Forward Delta

The forward delta, which we denote by Δ_f, is the sensitivity of the option price to a change in the forward. The forward delta is given by

$$\Delta_f \equiv \frac{\partial V_{BS}}{\partial f} = \lambda e^{-r_d \tau} N(\lambda d_1).$$

Unlike spot delta, where the call option holder simply sells Δ_{BS} of the base currency to hedge, if the option holder wishes to hedge using a forward contract, she would sell $e^{r_d \tau} \Delta_f$ of the forward contract. Intuitively, the reason for this is simply that the PnL from holding a position in a forward contract is not realized until a future date, and therefore needs to be discounted. More formally, consider a portfolio of long the call option with strike K and short X units of the forward with any strike. The value of the portfolio is

$$W_t = V_t - X F_t, \tag{10.6}$$

where $V_t = V_{BS}\left(f_t, t\right)$ and F_t is given by Equation (2.21). Then,

$$dW_t = \left(\frac{\partial V_{BS}}{\partial f} - X e^{-r_d \tau} \right) df_t + \text{further terms.}$$

To remove exposure to f_t, the trader must hedge by selling $X = e^{r_d \tau} \frac{\partial V_{BS}}{\partial f} = e^{r_d \tau} \Delta_f$ forward contracts.

10.2 THETA

$$\theta_{BS} \equiv \frac{\partial V_{BS}}{\partial t}$$

$$= \underbrace{-e^{-r_f \tau} \frac{n(d_1) S_t \sigma_{implied}}{2\sqrt{\tau}}}_{\text{1. Simple Theta.}} + \underbrace{\lambda \left[r_f S_t e^{-r_f \tau} N(\lambda d_1) - r_d K e^{-r_d \tau} N(\lambda d_2) \right]}_{\text{2. Forward Carry.}},$$

where $n(x)$ is the standard normal PDF. I split the formula for theta into two terms and discuss each of them in what follows.

Simple Theta   The reader will already have an understanding of this term because it behaves as described in Chapter 3. The three main features are as follows. First, the peak is $d_1 = 0$, or $S_t = Ke^{\frac{1}{2}\sigma^2_{implied}\tau}$, or $S_t \approx K$. Second, θ_{BS} is proportional to $\frac{1}{\tau}$ and so the theta of a longer dated option is smaller in magnitude than that of a shorter dated option. Third, theta is proportional to $\sigma_{implied}$, telling us that theta bills for expensive options are higher.

Forward Carry   The forward carry term did not appear in Chapter 3 because I had assumed that $r_f = r_d = 0$. In the presence of non-zero interest rates, the forward carry term appears and the theta of a call and put are no longer equal.

   To understand the intuition underlying forward carry let us take EUR-USD as an example once more and an option with expriy time T. At the time of writing, EUR interest rates are lower than USD interest rates, $r_f < r_d$. The forward is therefore said to be upward sloping, because $f_t = S_t e^{(r_d - r_f)\tau}$ is an increasing function of τ and $f_t > S_t$. As time progresses τ gets smaller and therefore the forward moves closer toward S_t.

   Recalling from Equation (10.4) that $f_t = \mathbb{E}[S_T]$ we see that as t progresses (τ diminishes), our expectation of S_T falls, all else being equal. This decreases the value of a call option and increases the value of a put option. This effect is known as forward carry and it is captured by term 2 above.

   We did not need to perform the algebraically tedious differentiation to extract term 2. To see how we can write it down immediately note that it can be rewritten as

$$r_f S_t \Delta_{BS} + r_d K \Delta_K. \tag{10.7}$$

Next, recall the interpretation that Δ_{BS} is the number of EUR that the option is equivalent to being long and Δ_K is the number of USD that the option is equivalent to being long (Δ_K is be negative for a EUR-USD call option) after accounting for the option premium. The PnL from holding Δ_{BS} EUR over a time period dt is $r_f S_t \Delta_{BS} dt$ USD, and the holding Δ_K USD yields $r_d K \Delta_K dt$ USD, resulting in Equation (10.7).

Forward Carry and the Carry Trade   The so-called *carry trade* is one of the oldest and most widely used strategies in FX. The basic idea is to borrow in the low-interest-rate currency and invest in the higher-interest-rate currency. In our example, this strategy would mean borrowing in EUR and investing in USD. If S_t remains unchanged, the PnL of the carry trade per EUR over time period dt in USD is

$$(r_d - r_f)S_t.$$

Equation (10.7) makes clear that the forward carry component of the theta of an option is approximately equivalent to implementing the carry trade. To understand this, consider a short ATMS call option, or long an ATMS put option without executing a delta hedge. Then, $\Delta_{BS} \approx -\Delta_K \approx -0.5$ and $S_t = K$. Equation (10.7) then reduces to approximately

$$-0.5(r_d - r_f)S_t.$$

Implementing the strategy with 2 EUR notional of the option for a period dt yields approximately the same PnL as the carry trade.

10.3 GAMMA

$$\Gamma_{BS} \equiv \frac{\partial \Delta_{BS}}{\partial S} = \frac{\partial^2 V_{BS}}{\partial S^2} = e^{-r_f \tau} \frac{n(d_1)}{S_t \sigma_{implied} \sqrt{\tau}}. \tag{10.8}$$

The formula for gamma confirms our analysis in Chapter 4. There are three points to recapitulate. First, the numerator is $n(d_1)$, which peaks when the strike is ATM. Second, gamma decreases when $\sigma_{implied}$ rises. Third, gamma is proportional to $\frac{1}{\sqrt{\tau}}$ and so shorter dated options have higher gamma than longer dated options.

Trader's gamma can be calculated in the context of BSM by applying Equation 4.3,

$$\Gamma_{BS,trader} = e^{-r_f \tau} \frac{n(d_1)}{100\sigma_{implied} \sqrt{\tau}}.$$

Using this equation it is straightforward to calculate gamma for an ATM option without using an option pricing software. For an ATM option, $d_1 = 0$. The trader should memorize $n(0) = 0.4$. It is then straightforward to calculate trader's gamma. For example, if $r_f = 0$, then for a 1-year expiry option with $\sigma_{implied} = 10\%$, $\Gamma_{BS,trader} = 4\%$. For example, if the trader buys 100 million notioanl of a 1-year EUR-USD option, and EUR-USD rises by 1%, then she should have sold approximately 4 million EUR.

10.4   VEGA

$$v_{BS} \equiv \frac{\partial V_{BS}}{\partial \sigma_{implied}} = S_t e^{-r_f \tau} \sqrt{\tau} n(d_1).\qquad(10.9)$$

The formula for vega confirms our analysis in Chapter 5. There are two points to recapitulate. First, the numerator is $n(d_1)$ which peaks when the strike is ATM. Second, vega is proportional to $\sqrt{\tau}$ and so shorter dated options have less vega than longer dated options.

Throughout this text, 2.1 has been a key number. It appeared in Section 1.5.1 in the context of breakevens, in Section 3.1.1 in the context of theta, and in Equation 5.3 in the context of BSM vega for an ATM option.

The previous equation tells us where this number originates from. Measuring time in calendar days n instead of years means we can write

$$v_{BS} = S_t e^{-r_f \tau} \sqrt{n} \left(\frac{n(d_1)}{\sqrt{365}} \right) = \frac{2.1}{100} S_t e^{-r_f \tau} \sqrt{n}$$

because $\frac{n(d_1)}{\sqrt{365}} = 0.021$ where $d_1 = 0$.

10.5   VANNA

$$\text{Vanna} = \frac{\partial}{\partial S}\left(\frac{\partial V_{BS}}{\partial \sigma_{implied}} \right) = -e^{-r_f \tau} n(d_1) \frac{d_2}{\sigma_{implied}}.\qquad(10.10)$$

There are two important points to note. Even though $n(d_1)$ is maximum when the option is ATM, d_2 is very small. Therefore, ATM options have little vanna and options traders must trade OTM options to gain vanna exposure, as discussed in Chapter 7.

Next, vanna is proportional to $\frac{1}{\sigma_{implied}}$. The intuition here is that when $\sigma_{implied}$ is high, the vega profile is flatter and wider, as discussed in Section 5.5. It therefore changes by a smaller amount for a given move in S_t.

10.6 VOLGAMMA

Finally,

$$\text{Volgamma} \equiv \frac{\partial^2 V_{BS}}{\partial \sigma^2_{implied}} = S e^{-r_f \tau} \sqrt{\tau} n(d_1) \frac{d_1 d_2}{\sigma_{implied}}. \qquad (10.11)$$

$d_1 = 0$ for an ATM option. Therefore the volgamma for an ATM option is zero.

10.7 TRADER'S SUMMARY

- Δ_{BS} depends on $N(\lambda d_1)$, which is close to the probability that the option expires ITM, $N(\lambda d_2)$.
- Δ_{BS} depends on f_t, because the higher f_t, the higher the probability that the option expires ITM.
- The ATM or DNS is $K = S_t e^{\frac{1}{2}\sigma^2_{implied}\tau}$.
- Δ_K is the probability of an ITM expiry, and also the delta from the perspective of an investor based in the base currency.
- The forward delta, Δ_f, is not the number of forward contracts that must be entered into to hedge because the PnL from forward trading must be discounted.
- Theta can be split into two terms. Simple theta was discussed in detail in Chapter 3.1. Forward carry relates to the interest rate differential between the two currencies underlying the option contract. It makes options behave much like the classic FX carry trade.

CHAPTER 11

Predictability and Mean Reversion

T he majority of the ideas presented in this text rest on the idea that the spot rate is a martingale (Equation (2.9)) and it therefore exhibits no mean reversion or autocorrelation. This leads to the variance of the PDF growing with time. This growth is linear in the case of IID returns. This book has presented options theory based on this assumption. The main purpose in this chapter is to provide some empirical evidence to support this idea.

11.1 THE PAST AND THE FUTURE

Are future FX rates predictable using past rates alone? Is there mean reversion? Upon first inspection, one may be forgiven for suggesting that these questions are overly simplistic. After all, market participants are continuously bombarded with far more information relevant for forming forecasts than just past FX rates. However, this question *is* important and interesting at least partly because options theory is built on the idea that the discounted spot process is a martingale, although under the risk-neutral probability measure. If the answer to the previous questions turns out to be *yes*, then there may exist exploitable profitable trading opportunities that take advantage of a misspecification in option pricing models. More generally, by studying this question, we learn whether the probability distributions that we use to model FX rates for the purpose of option pricing should incorporate some level of price-based predictability.

I begin by restating the question in probabilistic terms. This will allow us to construct a statistical test to apply to a set of historical FX data.

Let S_t denote the FX rate at time t and define the log return between time $t - \delta$ and t by

$$r_t^\delta \equiv \log \frac{S_t}{S_{t-\delta}}.$$

If the relation

$$\text{Corr}\left[f(r_s^\delta), r_{t+\delta}^\delta\right] = 0 \qquad (11.1)$$

for all t and $s \leq t$ holds for an arbitrary function $f(\cdot)$, then past prices cannot be used to forecast future returns. The intuition here is that there must be some correlation between the past, or some function of the past, and future returns to use the past to say anything about the future. Therefore, a probabilistic statement of our question is simply, does Equation (11.1) hold in historical FX data?

To study this question, I take as a starting point the special case of (11.1) in which $f(\cdot)$ is a linear function. If $f(\cdot)$ is linear, then in effect we are testing for the existence of autocorrelations. Relation (11.1) simplifies to

$$\text{Corr}\left[r_s^\delta, r_{t+\delta}^\delta\right] \equiv \frac{\mathbb{E}\left[r_s^\delta r_{t+\delta}^\delta\right] - \mathbb{E}\left[r_t^\delta\right]^2}{\mathbb{E}\left[(r_t^\delta)^2\right] - \mathbb{E}\left[r_t^\delta\right]^2} = 0. \qquad (11.2)$$

Testing (11.2) is the topic of the next section.

11.2 EMPIRICAL ANALYSIS

The aim in this section is to test the hypothesis that Equation (11.2) holds in historical FX data. This involves two steps. The first is to estimate the quantity $\text{Corr}[r_s^\Delta, r_{t+\Delta}^\Delta]$. This is straightforward; I replace the population moments in (11.2) with their sample counterparts.

The second step is to estimate the standard error of the estimate. The reason for this is that, even if the true autocorrelation in returns is zero, the estimated autocorrelation may not be zero.

Although the data set used in this analysis is relatively large, it is finite in size and so there may not be sufficiently many data points for the sample autocorrelation to converge to the value of its population counterpart. The standard error of the estimate provides a measure of the uncertainty associated with the autocorrelation estimate. Here, I do not reject relation (11.2) unless the estimate lies at least 1.96 standard deviations from zero. The number 1.96 is chosen because this corresponds to just a 5% chance that we reject (11.2) even if it is true. Using a number less than 1.96 would increase the chance of a false rejection, which is, of course, undesirable. Increasing this number further would decrease the chance of a rejection of (11.2) altogether. Nevertheless, the reader will see below that the implications of the statistics presented in this analysis are robust and relatively insensitive to the choice of rejection level.

Furthermore, to ensure that the results presented here are convincing, I calculate the standard errors using two separate techniques, a bootstrap method and a Generalized Method of Moments (GMM)-based method.

The empirical analysis uses daily FX rate data for the Japanese yen (JPY), British pound (GBP), Euro (EUR), Canadian dollar (CAD), Australian dollar (AUD), and Swiss Franc (CHF) all against the US dollar (USD). Accordingly, I set $\delta = 1$ day and take daily returns, $t = i\delta$ for $i = 1, \ldots, N$. Here, N denotes the data sample size. All the data samples end on 10 March 2011. However, N depends on the currency pair in question because the samples start on different dates.

WHY STUDY RETURNS RATHER THAN EXCHANGE RATES DIRECTLY?

Most empirical work uses returns because they are plausibly stationary over time. *Stationary* does not mean constant. It means that the joint distribution of $r_t^\delta, r_{t+j}^\delta$ depends only on j, and not on t, and the distribution of r_t^δ does not depend on t. The following example illustrates why this is important in empirical work. For convenience, we drop the δ superscript.

Suppose that our aim is to calculate the variance of returns,

$$\text{Var}[r_t] \equiv \mathbb{E}[r_t^2] - \mathbb{E}[r_t]^2.$$

To estimate the required population moments $\mathbb{E}[r_t^2]$ and $\mathbb{E}[r_t]$, one would typically take a time series of historical data, $r_1, r_2, \ldots, r_N$, and calculate the respective sample moments, $\frac{1}{N}\sum_{i=1}^N r_i^2$ and $\frac{1}{N}\sum_{i=1}^N r_i$. However, these sample moments clearly cannot converge to their population counterparts if r_1 were drawn from a distribution with a different mean and variance to r_2, and r_3 were drawn from a distribution with yet another mean and variance, and so on; we require

(Continued)

many samples from the same distribution. Stationarity implies each r_i is drawn from the same distribution so that

$$\mathbb{E}[r_t] = \text{constant for all } t. \tag{11.3}$$

$$\mathbb{E}[r_t^2] = \text{constant for all } t. \tag{11.4}$$

Stationarity (and some other conditions, for which I refer the reader to Singleton, 2006) allow sample moments calculated over time to converge to their population counterparts.

Exchange rates themselves are unlikely to be stationary variables. First, their variance grows with time. One is more sure of the USD-JPY exchange rate tomorrow than of this exchange rate in a year's time; the variance of S_1 is smaller than that of S_{365}. This violates a condition analogous to (11.4) since $\mathbb{E}[S_t^2]$ depends on t.

Second, exchange rates may tend to rise or fall with time depending on, among other things, inflation and interest rate differentials between currencies. Such a tendencies violate the analogous condition to (11.3) since $\mathbb{E}[S_t]$ depends on t.

A final point to note is that stationarity forces only unconditional distribution of returns to remain unchanged over time. The conditional distribution may change.

The fixed exchange rate mechanism broke down in early 1973. Accordingly, the JPY, GBP and CHF series begin on 1 June 1973 ($N = 9854$). The CAD series starts a year later on 1 June 1974 because CAD was held essentially at parity with USD for several months after the demise of Bretton Woods ($N = 9594$). The EUR series starts on 1 January 1999, when it replaced the Deutsche Mark and several other European currencies ($N = 3179$). Finally, the AUD series starts on 9 December 1983 when it was first allowed to float freely ($N = 7109$). We take $s = t - j\Delta$ for $j = 1, 2, \ldots, d$ to test for autocorrelations lagging up to and including d days.

For convenience, I rewrite (11.2) as a function of the population moments:

$$\text{Corr}\left[r_s^{\Delta}, r_{t+\Delta}^{\Delta}\right] = g(\mu), \tag{11.5}$$

where μ is the vector,

$$\mu \equiv \left[\mathbb{E}[r_t^{\Delta}] \quad \mathbb{E}[(r_t^{\Delta})^2] \quad \mathbb{E}[r_s^{\Delta} r_{t+\Delta}^{\Delta}]\right]$$

and

$$g(\mu) \equiv \frac{\mu_3 - \mu_1^2}{\mu_2 - \mu_1^2}.$$

Here, μ_i refers to the ith element in μ. Next, I estimate $\mathrm{Corr}\left[r_s^{\Delta}, r_{t+\Delta}^{\Delta}\right]$ by replacing the population moments in (11.5) with their sample counterparts:

$$\widehat{\mathrm{Corr}}\left[r_s^{\Delta}, r_{t+\Delta}^{\Delta}\right] \equiv g(\hat{\mu}),$$

where

$$\hat{\mu} \equiv \left[\frac{1}{N-j}\sum_{i=j+1}^{N} r_{i\Delta}^{\Delta} \quad \frac{1}{N-j}\sum_{i=j+1}^{N} (r_{i\Delta}^{\Delta})^2 \quad \frac{1}{N-j}\sum_{i=j+1}^{N} r_{i\Delta-j\Delta}^{\Delta}r_{i\Delta}^{\Delta}\right].$$

I calculate autocorrelations to 261 lags, allowing us to test if the returns on a particular date can tell us something about the returns on the same date in the following year. There are too many results to present in full here, but they are well summarized by Figure 11.1.

I have not been able to find statistically significant autocorrelations in the data. This holds true across all the currencies in question.

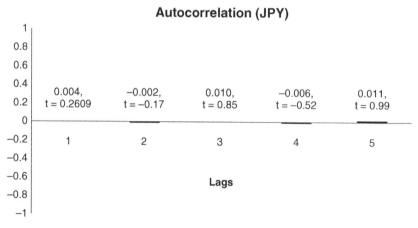

FIGURE 11.1 Autocorrelations in daily JPY data to 5 lags and the corresponding t-statistics. The t-statistic is defined as the ratio of the sample autocorrelation and the standard error of the estimate. This number should exceed 1.96 for the calculated autocorrelation to be statistically significant to the 5% level. We are unable to find evidence for statistically significant autocorrelation in any of the currency pairs used in the analysis. The t-statistics shown above are calculated using a GMM method. The results using the bootstrap method are very similar.

Only approximately 5% of the 1566 calculated autocorrelations were statistically significant, corresponding well to the 5% significance level used in the analysis. Our answer to the question posed in this chapter is therefore simply that we cannot find evidence that past returns can be used to predict future returns. This answer holds regardless of whether the GMM or bootstrap method is used to calculate the standard errors. These findings lend support to the martingale assumption used to price FX options.

Probability

The mathematics that underly options theory can appear imposing. However, the real challenges in practical options trading and risk management are conceptual, not mathematical. I do presume some exposure to undergraduate-level probability, statisics, and calculus. However, this appendix is written to provide a refresher on these topics via simple, example-based explanations of the mathematical concepts in the main text for readers who may have lost familiarity with these topics over the course of time. This appendix should be sufficient to keep this textbook self-contained.

A.1 PROBABILITY DENSITY FUNCTIONS (PDFS)

A.1.1 Discrete Random Variables and PMFs

Before studying PDFs, let us begin with probability mass functions (PMFs). PMFs provide a helpful introduction to PDFs, because they are the discrete state analogs of PDFs.

The EUR-USD spot rate at a future time T, S_T, is a random variable. Suppose that it can take one of three discrete values, 1.37, 1.39, and 1.41. Suppose also that the probabilies with which these values occur are

$$\Pr(S_T = 1.37) = 0.2$$
$$\Pr(S_T = 1.39) = 0.5$$
$$\Pr(S_T = 1.41) = 0.3.$$

The PMF belonging to S_T is shown in Figure A.1. It is a plot of the probability with which EUR-USD takes each of its possible values at T.

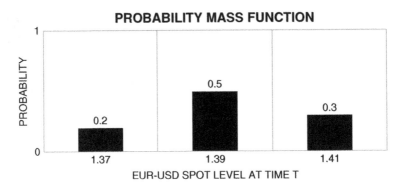

FIGURE A.1 The figure shows the PMF of S_T. In this case, S_T can take one of three discrete values. The PMF gives us the probability that S_T takes each of these values.

We have shown three states here, but we can extend this idea to many discrete states.

The expected value of S_T, denoted $\mathbb{E}[S_T]$, is calculated as follows.

$$\mathbb{E}[S_T] = \sum_{x \in X} x \Pr(S_T = x) \tag{A.1}$$

$$= \Pr(S_T = 1.37) \times 1.37 + \Pr(S_T = 1.39) \times 1.39 + \Pr(S_T = 1.41) \times 1.41$$

$$= 0.2 \times 1.37 + 0.5 \times 1.39 + 0.3 \times 1.41$$

$$= 1.3920,$$

where $X = \{1.37, 1.39, 1.41\}$. In words, the expectation of S_T is the weighted average value of S_T, with the weights given by the PMF.

If we wished to extend this idea to infinitely many, or a continuum of, states, then we must turn to PDFs. This is the topic of the next subsection.

A.1.2 Continuous Random Variables and PDFs

Next, suppose that S_T can take a continuum of values. The probability that S_T is between value a and b at time T is given by

$$\Pr(a < S_T \leq b) = \int_a^b f_{S_T}(x)\mathrm{d}x, \tag{A.2}$$

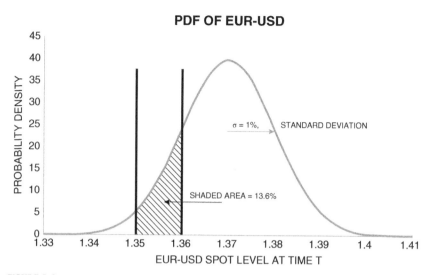

FIGURE A.2   The line shows the probability density function (of EUR-USD spot at time T in this example), $f_{S_T}(x)$. Suppose we wish to calculate the probability that EUR-USD is between $a = 1.35$ and $b = 1.36$ at time T. This is found by calculating the shaded area under the PDF, $\int_a^b f_{S_T}(x)\mathrm{d}x$, which is 13.6% in our example, assuming a normal distribution with zero mean and standard deviation $\sigma = 1\%$. See Section A.1.3 for more on normal distributions.

where $f_{S_T}(x)$ is the probability density function belonging to S_T. In words, there is a function $f_{S_T}(x)$, and the area underneath this function between a and b provides the probability that S_T will lie between a and b. Figure A.2 and its caption explain this idea.

The cumulative density function, or CDF, is denoted by $F_{S_T}(b)$ and it is the probability that $S_T \leq b$. That is,

$$F_{S_T}(b) = \Pr(S_T \leq b) = \int_{-\infty}^{b} f_{S_T}(x)\mathrm{d}x.$$

For option contracts, spot rates are rounded to the nearest pip. Therefore, strictly speaking, they take discrete rather than continuous values. However, the reason that practitioners apply PDFs rather than PMFs in their modeling is that, quite simply, there are a lot of pips! For example,

EUR-USD is rounded to four decimal places and so to specify just the probabilities of spot landing between 1.3500 and 1.3900, the modeler would have to specify 401 bars on a chart similar to Figure A.1. It is more convenient to treat the spot rate as a continuum and then specify $f_{S_T}(x)$. Then, if we wish to calculate the probability that EUR-USD expires at exactly 1.3700, we can apply Equation (A.2), setting $a = 1.36995$ and $b = 1.37004$.

Analogous to the PMF, the expected value of S_T is calculated as follows,

$$\mathbb{E}[S_T] = \int_{-\infty}^{\infty} x f_{S_T}(x) dx.$$

A.1.3   Normal and Log-normal Distributions

The normal distribution has two parameters, a mean and a standard derivation, or variance. If S_T is normally distributed, I denote it as

$$S_T \sim \mathcal{N}(\mu, \sigma^2).$$

Here, μ is the mean of S_T and σ is its standard deviation (σ^2 is its variance). That is,

$$\mu = \mathbb{E}[S_T],$$
$$\sigma^2 = \mathbb{E}[(S_T - \mu)^2].$$

The PDF of S_T is given by

$$f_{S_T}(x) = \frac{1}{\sqrt{2\pi\sigma^2}} \exp\left(-\frac{(x-\mu)^2}{2\sigma^2}\right). \tag{A.3}$$

$f_{S_T}(x)$ is shown in Figure A.3.

There are two important points to note relating to Equation (A.3). The first is that the peak of $f_{S_T}(x)$ occurs at $x = \mu$. The second, is that the probability that $-\sigma < S_T < \sigma$ is 0.68. That is, using our result from Section A.1.2,

$$\int_{-\sigma}^{\sigma} f_{S_T}(x) = \int_{-\sigma}^{\sigma} \frac{1}{\sqrt{2\pi\sigma^2}} \exp\left(-\frac{(x-\mu)^2}{2\sigma^2}\right) = 0.68. \tag{A.4}$$

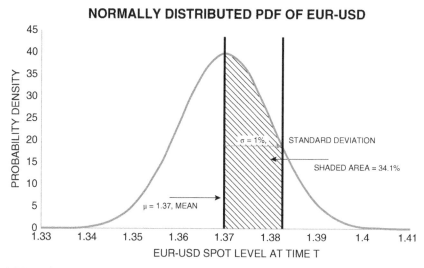

FIGURE A.3 The figure draws the function from Equation (A.3) for EUR-USD using $\sigma = 1\%$ and $\mu = 1.37$. The area contained within $\mu \pm \sigma = 68\%$. Therefore the probability that the EUR-USD spot rate is $1.37 \pm 1\%$ is 68%.

If S_T is log-normally distributed, I denote it as

$$\ln S_T \sim \mathcal{N}(\mu, \sigma^2).$$

The important point to note is that S_T can now never be negative. Indeed, this is one of the primary reasons that the log-normal distribution was applied in securities modeling rather than the normal distribution.

There are two important points for readers to note. First, when σ is low then under the log-normal distribution the spot price behaves in a manner very similar to the normal distribution. This is illustrated in Figure A.4. This is also the reason that the early chapters in this book explain the main concepts in options theory using normal distributions.

Second, as σ increases the log-normal and normal distributions deviate, as shown in Figure A.5. The normal distribution is symmetric and therefore remains positive for negative values of the spot rate. The log-normal distribution allows only positive values for the spot rate, and it does so by devloping a positive skewness. That is, it puts the weight that the normal distribution has in the left tail, into an extended right tail. The peak also shifts to the left.

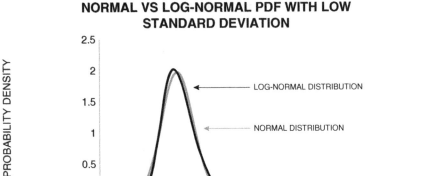

FIGURE A.4 The black line shows a log-normal distribution and the gray line shows a normal distribution setting $\mu = 1$ and $\sigma = 0.2$. Since σ is (relatively) small, the normal distribution and log-normal distribution are distinguishable by only a small amount.

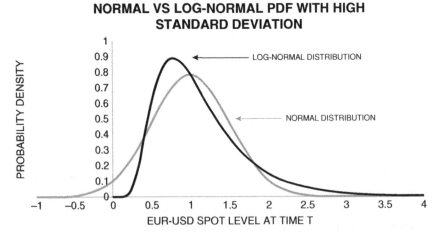

FIGURE A.5 The gray line shows the normal distribution and the black line shows a log-normal distribution with $\mu = 1$ and $\sigma = 0.5$. Since σ is large, the lines deviate from one another. While the normal distribution remains symmetric, and remains positive for negative values of EUR-USD spot, the log-normal distribution develops a positive skewness and does not allow probability that EUR-USD goes negative.

Calculus

This section provides a short refresher of the concept of a partial derivative.

Denote the option valuation function by $V(S, \sigma, t)$. In order to calculate the option price we insert the value of spot S, volatility σ and time t into a function V and it returns a price. We wish to understand how V changes if any one of S, σ, or t change while the other two variables remain constant.

Suppose that $S = S_t$ and $\sigma = \sigma_t$. The change in the option price ΔV due to S moving from S_t to $S_t + \delta$ is

$$\Delta V = V(S_t + \delta, \sigma_t, t) - V(S_t, \sigma_t, t).$$

Therefore, the change in the option price per unit move in S is

$$\frac{\Delta V}{\delta} = \frac{V(S_t + \delta, \sigma_t, t) - V(S_t, \sigma_t, t)}{\delta}. \tag{B.1}$$

Taking the limit as $\delta \to 0$ we have the *partial* derivative of the option price with respect to S, evaluated when $S = S_t$.

$$\frac{\partial V(S, \sigma, t)}{\partial S}\Big|_{S=S_t} \equiv \lim_{\delta \to 0} \frac{V(S_t + \delta, \sigma_t, t) - V(S_t, \sigma_t, t)}{\delta}.$$

If S moves from S_t to a new level S_1 while σ (and t) remain unchanged, then the new value of the option is

$$V(S_1, \sigma_t, t) = V(S_t, \sigma_t, t) + \frac{\partial V(S, \sigma, t)}{\partial S}\Big|_{S=S_t} \times (S_1 - S_t) + \text{higher-order terms}.$$

This approximation is generally more accurate as $S_t - S_t$ gets smaller.

There are at least three important points to remember. First, the partial derivative provides the sensitivity of the function to one of the variables changing while holding the others fixed. Earlier, we allowed S to change, but we could equally have allowed σ to change. Second, the partial derivative is accurate to first order, or infinitesimally small moves in S only. For larger moves, one must treat the previous calculation as an approximation only, or include higher-order terms. Third, the partial derivative is itself (in genaral) a function of the variables (S and σ in the previous example). It is therefore important to note where the partial derivative is evaluated.

Glossary

ATM	At-the-money
ATMS	At-the-money spot
BOJ	Bank of Japan
BSM	Black-Scholes-Merton
CDF	Cumulative density function
DNS	Delta neutral straddle
FVA	Forward volatility agreement
FX	Foreign exchange
ITM	In-the-money
OTC	Over the counter
OTM	Out-of-the-money
PDE	Partial differential equation
pip	Price interest point
PDF	Probability density function
SNB	Swiss National Bank

References

Bjork, T. (2009), "Arbitrage theory in continuous time," Oxford Finance.

Black, F. & Scholes, M. (1973), "The pricing of options and corporate liabilities," *Journal of Political Economy* **81**(3), 637.

Bollerslev, T. (1986), "Generalized autoregressive conditional heteroskedasticity," *Journal of Econometrics* **31**, 307–327.

Cochrane, J. H. (2005), *Asset Pricing (Revised Edition)*, Princeton University Press.

Duffie, D. (2001), "Dynamic asset pricing theory," Princeton University Press.

Engle, R. (1982), "Autoregressive conditional heteroskedasticity with estimates of the variance of united kingdom inflation," *Econometrica* **50**, 987–1007.

Garman, M. B. & Kohlhagen, S. W. (1983), "Foreign currency option values," *Journal of International Money and Finance* **2**(3), 231.

Gatheral, J. (2006), *The Volatility Surface—A Practitioner's Guide*, John Wiley and Sons.

Hull, J. C. (2011), "Options, futures and other derivatives," Pearson.

Campbell, A. W. L. & Mackinlay, A. C. (1997), *The Econometrics of Financial Markets*, Princeton University Press.

Kozhan, R., Neuberger, A., & Schneider, P. (2013), "The skew risk premium in the equity index market," *Review of Financial Studies* **26**(9), 2174–2203.

Merton, R. C. (1973), "Theory of rational option pricing," *Bell Journal of Economics and Management Science* **4**(1), 141.

Neuberger, A. (2012), "Realized skewness," *Review of Financial Studies* **25**(11), 3423–3455.

Rebonato, R. (2004), "Volatility and correlation: The perfect hedger and the fox."

Shreve, S. E. (2000), "Stochastic calculus for finance II: Continuous-time models," Springer.

Singleton, K. J. (2006), *Empirical Dynamic Asset Pricing: Model Specification and Econometric Assessment*, Princeton University Press.

Zhang, L., Mykland, P. A., & Ait-Sahalia, Y. (2005), "A tale of two time scales: Determining integrated volatility with noisy high-frequency data," *American Statistical Association* **100**(472), 1394.

Index

Printed and bound by CPI Group (UK) Ltd, Croydon, CR0 4YY

16/04/2025

14658451-0002